F·O·R·M·U·L·A

Student's Book

JANET OLEARSKI · RON WHITE · EDDIE WILLIAMS

MACMILLAN
PUBLISHERS

FORMULA 2

Contents

LESSON 1

He's a Jack-of-All-Trades

Meg and Lisa work at the Ocean Institute. Meg is a scientist there. Lisa is a graduate student. She is from Holland.

Meg Hi, Lisa. Busy?
Lisa Hi, Meg. Yes, pretty busy. I'm doing a cookery course at the tech. It's two evenings a week.
Meg Really. So, you're interested in cooking, are you?
Lisa Oh, yes. I'm learning to cook Indian food. We've got an Indian teacher, and she's a real enthusiast.
Meg I love Indian food.
Lisa And do you like cooking it?
Meg No, not really, but I enjoy eating it.
Lisa Oh, by the way, who was that man in your office yesterday?
Meg Which man? What did he look like?
Lisa Tall, athletic. Very tanned. Grey, straight hair.
Meg Oh, that's Jack Craig. He's from Sydney. He's an old friend of Geoffrey's. He's been at sea for six months, on an expedition to the Caribbean.
Lisa What's his job?
Meg He's a Jack-of-all-trades.
Lisa What do you mean?
Meg Well, he does everything. He's very versatile. Come and meet him tomorrow.
Lisa Yes, I'd like to meet a Jack-of-all-trades. And I don't know any Australians.
Meg Well, this is your chance to meet one.

Exercise 1

The sentences below are not correct. Copy from the dialogue the sentences which give the correct answer.

1 Meg doesn't enjoy eating Indian food.
2 Lisa's teacher doesn't like teaching.
3 Lisa goes to classes once a week.
4 Jack is from the Caribbean.
5 Jack does very few things.

Exercise 2

When talking about our interests and likes, we use patterns A and B. Complete the gaps in the tables with words from the dialogue.

Pattern A	
I am interested in I am not interested in	________ cooking.

Pattern B	
I like I don't like I enjoy I don't enjoy	________ ________ ________ ________

Complete the rules by filling in the blanks.

Rule: After 'be interested in', 'like' and 'enjoy', we use verb + ________, e.g.

I ________ interested in cooking.

like ________

________ sailing.

Complete pattern C with words from the dialogue.

Pattern C	
I'm learning	________ Indian food.

'Learn' + 'to' + ________ means learning how to do something. So, Lisa is learning how ____ ________ Indian food.

Complete these sentences with the correct verb from the list.

1 Lisa is interested in ________ Jack.
2 Lisa isn't learning ________ Chinese food.
3 Lisa's teacher enjoys ________ the evening class.
4 We are interested in ________ English.
5 I am learning ________ English.

to cook   to speak   teaching   learning   meeting

Exercise 3

Practise this dialogue with a partner and then make similar dialogues with your partner. Use the words to help you. Take turns at being A and B.

A: Who was that (1) woman in your car?
B: Which (2) woman? What did (3) she look like?
A: (4) Short, pretty. Very fair, with long straight hair.
B: Oh, that's (5) Anne Balmain. She's from France.
A: I'd like to meet (6) her.
B: Sure. Let me introduce you.

(1) man in your office?   (2) man?

(3) he look like?

(4) Tall, athletic. Very tanned, with short curly hair.; Average height. Dark with short straight hair.; Average height. Fair with short grey hair.

(5) Jim Bond. He's from Australia.; Pat Hornby. She's from England.; Doug Landers. He's from America.

(6) him

Exercise 4

Complete the sentences below about yourself. Here is some extra vocabulary to help you.

Verbs
play, watch cook, eat listen

Things and Activities	
sport	football, baseball, etc.
food	Italian, French, etc.
TV programmes	soap operas, documentaries, etc.
music	classical, pop, jazz, folk, etc.

I would like to introduce myself. My name is ________ and I am interested in ________. I like ________ and I enjoy ________, but I don't like ________. I am learning ________.

We Used to Be a Busy Organization

MEMO

University of Wessex

From: Dr J R Leafe
Vice-Chancellor

To: Dr G Walton
Director, Ocean Institute

You are doubtless aware that the National Universities Finance Committee recently visited our University and they investigated our financial situation.

In the past, the University Central Fund used to provide the Institute with half a million pounds a year and the fund still contributes to the Institute. However, it cannot continue to contribute because it does not have the resources.

I am sorry about this ultimatum, but my hands are tied. The University used to have plenty of money. Now we have very little, but we still have many expenses. So, you must find £500 000 by next April, or close.

JRL

JRL

From: G Walton, Director

To: All Staff

I have received an ultimatum from the V-C. He says that we must find half a million pounds or close.

You will realize that this is not exactly a surprise. In the past, we were a very busy organization and there used to be several expeditions a year. For instance, five years ago, we organized expeditions to the South Pacific, the Red Sea, the Antarctic and Norway. Two years ago, we ran four expeditions. This year we have still one expedition to the Caribbean, but we have no expeditions for next year.

The most important change is in our University funding. We used to receive money from the University, but because it has financial problems, it isn't going to give us any money. The result is that whereas we used to have many small financial problems, we now have one very big problem.

Unless we find £500 000 by April, the University will close the Institute. I am very worried. Any ideas?

G.W.

GW

Exercise 1

Choose True or False. Then write the sentences from the text which give the answers.

1 The Institute used to receive nothing from the University.
2 The University has a lot of money.
3 Five years ago there were four expeditions.
4 The Institute has a very small financial problem.
5 The Institute will close unless it can find half a million pounds.

Exercise 2

Complete with words from the text.

1 The University Central Fund ________ the Institute with half a million pounds a year.
2 The Central Fund ________ contributes to the Institute.
3 The University cannot ________ to contribute.
4 The University ________ plenty of money.

Complete the rule.

Rule: When we refer to a continuous state or repeated events in a past period which is now completed, we use '________ to' + verb. 'Used to' often contrasts a ________ state or repeated events in the ________ with states or events in the present.

Example: *I used to get up very early.*
I get up later nowadays.

Interrogative (normally):	Did I use to . . . . . ? (Did you use to . . . . . ?, etc.)
Negative (normally):	I didn't use to . . . . . (You didn't use to . . . . ., etc.)
Negative Interrogative:	Didn't I use to . . . . . ? (Didn't you use to . . . . . ? etc.)

Complete these sentences with the verbs given below.

1 Lisa ________ to work by bicycle and she still ________.
2 The University ________ plenty of money, but nowadays it ________ very little money.
3 The Institute ________ small financial problems, but now it ________ a very big one.
4 Everyone at the Institute ________ happy, but now they ________ worried.

used to travel; has; runs; cycles; are; used to be; used to have

Exercise 3

Here are two people comparing past and present habits. Some habits are still the same, but some are different.

Habits	**Past**	**Present**
	I used to go by bus.	Nowadays I go by tube.

Practise the dialogue with a partner, taking turns to be A and B.

A: What time do you get up?
B: Half past six, but I used to get up at seven.
A: I used to get up at six, but I get up later nowadays. How do you go to work?
B: I go by bus. I used to drive. And you?
A: I used to go by bus, but now I go by tube.

Part of the table below has been completed for speaker A as an example. Complete this table for yourself. Then talk with your partner about your past and present habits. Use the patterns above.

	Past	**Present**
Get up	6	7 o'clock
Go to work	by bus	by tube
Have dinner		
Go to bed		

Exercise 4

Here is part of an article on people's habits. Write a similar article about yourself and your partner, substituting information about yourselves from Exercise 3.

We asked people about their past and present habits. Many people wrote to us. Some habits are different, some are still the same.

For instance, whereas Dutch student Lisa Anders used to get up at seven o'clock, now she gets up at six thirty. All people agree that getting up early isn't much fun.

And what about going to work? Geoff Walton, Director of the Ocean Institute, used to drive to work but now he goes by tube, whereas his colleague, Meg Brooke, still drives.

As to dinner times, Australian Jack Craig says whereas he used to eat at nine or ten o'clock, now he has dinner at seven thirty. Most people have dinner by eight o'clock.

LESSON 3

We Wanted to Go There

Lisa, Jack and Meg are talking about Jack's trip to the Caribbean.

Jack Anyway, the Caribbean was great.
Lisa How marvellous! Did you go to Cuba?
Jack No, I wanted to go there, but I couldn't.
Lisa Why not?
Jack We couldn't get visas. So we went to Haiti instead. We stayed there for a week, and then we returned to Barbados.
Lisa Haiti. How fascinating. Did you see a voodoo ceremony? I've always wanted to see one.
Jack No, we wanted to go to one, but we couldn't.
Lisa What a pity.
Meg Anyway, Lisa, I think that there has been a voodoo on the Institute for some time.
Lisa Why? What's the matter?
Meg Geoff says we used to be very busy, but now we've got no expeditions and we're broke. The Vice-Chancellor says we must raise half a million pounds by April next year – or close!
Lisa But, how can we get that amount of money?
Meg I don't know. Geoff wants to find sponsors to give us some money.
Lisa Ah, I see. Like the man who wanted to cycle round the world. He obtained sponsors – a bank and a cycle company, I think. They gave him money for his expedition.
Meg Yes, but we're an *Ocean* Institute, Lisa.
Lisa I know, but what about *sailing* around the world?
Jack What a good idea! But we need a boat. Now, let me think.

Exercise 1

Use words from the dialogue to answer these questions.

1 Why didn't Jack go to Cuba?
2 Where did he go instead?
3 Why didn't he see a voodoo ceremony?
4 Why does Meg think there's been a voodoo on the Institute?
5 What does Geoff want to find?
6 What did the cyclist's sponsors do?

Exercise 2

Find four examples of this pattern in the dialogue.

'want to' + verb

Find one example of this pattern.

'could' + 'not' + verb.

Complete these sentences with the above patterns.

1 Jack ________ Cuba, but he ________ there because he ________ a visa.
2 Jack is interested in voodoo. He ________ a ceremony, but he ________.
3 Lisa has always ________ to a voodoo ceremony.
4 The Institute is broke, so Geoff ________ sponsors to get some money.
5 A man who ________ round the world obtained money from some sponsors.

Now write three sentences about things that you *wanted to do* and three reasons why you *couldn't* do them.

Exercise 3

Practise this dialogue with a partner. Take turns at being A and B. Then add some information of your own and practise the dialogue again.

A: Hello, how was your vacation?
B: We wanted to (1) go to Stonehenge.
A: Oh, why couldn't you (2) go there?
B: (3) We didn't have time.
A: Oh, that was too bad. Perhaps next time (4) you'll have more time.
B: I hope so!

(1) visit the National Gallery; see the new Andrew Lloyd Webber musical; stay at the Meridien; dine at Le Gavroche

(2) visit it? see it? stay there? dine there?

(3) It was closed; We couldn't get tickets; It was fully booked; We couldn't afford it.

(4) it will be open; you'll have better luck; it won't be full; you'll have more money

Exercise 4

Last weekend everything went wrong when some visitors came to stay with you. Complete this postcard to another friend about your unsuccessful weekend. Use words and phrases from Exercise 3. You can also add some more information of your own.

Last weekend everything went wrong.
(Name of friends) came to stay. They wanted to go to (famous place) but we couldn't because ________. So, we changed our plans. (Name of friends) also wanted to visit (name of museum) but ________.
Then (name of friend) said, 'Let's see (name of play or film).' That was a great idea. We all wanted ________ it, but we ________ tickets.
So, in the end we stayed at home and watched television.
I hope that next time we'll ________!

LESSON 4

I Like Sailing

Exercise 1

Choose True or False. Then write the sentences from the text which give the answers.

1 Bergman will lend Meg a boat.
2 Bergman wants publicity for his boatyard.
3 Jack is very happy about the boat.
4 Fifteen people have applied for the expedition.
5 Yolanda is American.
7 Geoff and Meg decide to take Yolanda.

Exercise 2

Study the examples and the rule.

Examples:

Yolanda has been a photographer for six years.
Is she a photographer now? Yes.
Yolanda was a student for three years.
Is she a student now? No.

Rule: We can use 'have/has been' (the Present Perfect) when something continues from the past to the present.

(NB Exception 'have been to' = visited in the past, eg *I've been to Japan.*)

Rewrite 1 to 8, with the information given. Use '*has been* . . . *for*' or '*was* . . . *for*'.

Example:

Peter/a racing driver/1988 until now.
Peter *has been* a racing driver for 2 years.
(if 'now' is 1990)
Lisa/a student/1983 until 1988
Lisa *was* a student for 5 years.

1 Geoffrey/a teacher/1970 until 1976.
2 Jack/a sailor/1975 until 1980.
3 Meg/a student/1976 until 1980.
4 Meg/a scientist/1980 until now.
5 Geoffrey/Director of the Institute/1977 until now.
6 Lisa/at school/from 1980 to 1987.
7 Otto Bergman/the owner of the boatyard/six months (until now).
8 Yolanda/a photographer/1983 until now.

Exercise 3

'I *have* a proposition *to make*'. Use the same structure to finish the exchanges. Choose from the verbs in the list below.

1 Yolanda's busy. She has a letter . . . . .
2 Listen! Lisa has an idea . . . . .
3 Lisa's going to be busy. She has a lot of food . . . . .
4 Geoff and Meg are busy. They have a lot of applicants . . . . .
5 Geoff and Meg also have a lot of details . . . . .
6 Yolanda has some more photographs . . . . .
7 Meg can't come now. She has an important telephone call . . . . .

to take, to write, to discuss, to interview, to suggest, to make, to cook

Exercise 4

Write a letter describing yourself. Say what you like and don't like, and also use sentences with

'*have been a* . . . . . *for* . . . . .' or '*was a* . . . . . *for* . . . . .'

LESSON 5

It's the Camera I Bought Last Summer

Dorothy Walton is talking to her husband's secretary, Suzy.

Dorothy Are these your photographs, Suzy?
Suzy Yes, they're the photos that we took at the yachting marina on Friday.
Dorothy May I have a look?
Suzy Yes, of course. Here are the ones that I took, and these are the ones that Yolanda took.
Dorothy Yolanda?
Suzy Yolanda Richmond. She's the woman Meg and Dr Walton interviewed last week.
Dorothy I remember her. She's the tall, attractive, black girl I met in Geoffrey's office. The photos she took are excellent. They're so clear, aren't they? Is your camera new?
Suzy No, it's the camera that I bought last summer. It's the one that I always use.
Dorothy May I see the other photos?
Suzy Yes, but they're not very clear, I'm afraid.
Dorothy Mm. . . This is the woman I saw in the Institute last Thursday, isn't it?
Suzy Actually it's not a woman. It's a man.
Dorothy Oh, I see. Who is it?
Suzy It's Otto Bergman. He's lending us the yacht.
Dorothy Is this a picture of the yacht?
Suzy No, it's not. It's the car that we hired.
Dorothy Is it? May I borrow your magnifying glass?
Suzy Have a look at this photo, Mrs Walton. It's clearer.
Dorothy Oh, is this the lovely little dog that you found in the park?
Suzy No, Mrs Walton, it's not the dog. It's your husband. It's Dr Walton.
Dorothy Suzy, your birthday's in September, isn't it?
Suzy Yes. Why?
Dorothy I'm going to buy you an automatic camera. Your photos are terrible. I can't even recognize the man I'm married to.

Exercise 1

Read the dialogue and complete the sentences.

1 It's the camera ________________________.
2 ____________ we took at the yachting marina.
3 Is this the lovely little dog ________________?
4 ________________________________ we hired.
5 ____________________ I met in Geoffrey's office.
6 She's the woman ________________________.
7 ________________________ I saw in the Institute.

Exercise 2

Match the sentences.

1 This is the camera.
2 Where's the electrician?
3 These are the letters.
4 He's the journalist.
5 This is the gold watch.
6 She's the businesswoman.

a) You forgot to post *them*.
b) He met *her* in Münich.
c) We saw *it* in the jeweller's.
d) I asked *him* to mend the washing machine.
e) They don't like *him*.
f) She bought *it* last summer.

Now join the sentences with 'that', but leave out the word in *italics*, like this:

1 This is the camera. She bought *it* last summer.
This is the camera that she bought last summer.

Rule: We can use a relative clause when we want to give more information about a noun. When we are talking about people, animals or things, we can begin the relative clause with 'that'. We can sometimes omit 'that'.

Exercise 3

Practise the dialogue with a partner and then make up similar dialogues, using the words below.

A: What's that?
B: It's the (1) report I wrote.
A: May I (2) see it?
B: Yes, of course. It's the one (3) I researched for the company.
A: May I (4) read it at home?
B: Yes, certainly.

(1) postcard I got from Suzy; computer I bought for my nephew; book I read; old jumper I had in the cupboard

(2) look at it? try it? read it? wear it?

(3) she sent from Madrid; I don't know how to operate; I borrowed from the library; I sent to the cleaner's

(4) show it to the others? look at the instructions? keep it until next week? wear it on Saturday?

Exercise 4

Think of five things that you own or that you are wearing. Write about them, like this:

It's something (that) I got for my birthday.
It's something (that) I bought for my English lesson.

Ask your partner to guess what the things are. Write sentences like this:

You're thinking of the tie (that) you got for your birthday.
You're thinking of the book (that) you bought for your English lesson.

LESSON 6

The Yacht Will Be Ideal

Dr Walton is writing to Otto Bergman, the owner of the yacht construction company.

The International Ocean Institute
32 Carlton Square Gardens
London SW1 3NS

May 19th

Dear Otto,

It was a pleasure to meet you on Friday. The yacht looks splendid and will be ideal for the expedition.

You wanted to know about our progress so far. Well, we'll make our final selection of the crew when Meg returns from the Oceanographic Conference in Florida. We've interviewed fourteen candidates already, but only one or two are suitable. We'll definitely choose Yolanda Richmond. (She's the photographer you met on Friday.) She's determined and reliable. Her photos of the voyage will bring us plenty of publicity. We'll take Lisa Anders too. She's our most talented research student, and she's an excellent cook. She'll be able to help Meg with her scientific reports. Jack Craig is the most experienced male candidate. You'll meet him when he comes to see the yacht on Tuesday. He has worked on boats all his life and he can repair anything. I know because I used to share a flat with him in Hong Kong.

Meg and I will plan the route as soon as we've got a complete crew, and we'll inform the press when everything is ready. We'll need the yacht as soon as we have the money from our sponsors. I'll phone you when they confirm everything.

Until then,

Kindest regards,

Geoffrey

Geoffrey

Exercise 1

Choose True or False.

1 The yacht will be ideal for the expedition.
2 Otto Bergman will meet Jack Craig on Thursday.
3 Meg is in Florida.
4 Yolanda's photos have brought them plenty of publicity.
5 Meg and Dr Walton have planned the route.
6 When the sponsors have confirmed everything, Dr Walton will phone Otto.

Exercise 2

Read the example and then complete these sentences.

Example:

I *shall order* lunch as soon as my friend *arrives*. (order/arrive)

1 You ________ him when he ________ you on Tuesday. (meet/visit)
2 He ________ television when he ________ home. (watch/get)
3 She ________ us as soon as the baby ________ ___. (phone/be born)
4 We ________ as soon as we ________ the results of the exam. (write/hear)
5 The police ________ you as soon as they ________ your car. (inform/find)

Rule: We use the verb with 'will' or 'shall' in the first part of the sentence, but after 'when' or ________ we use the Present Simple.

Exercise 3

Read Meg's notes on her trip to Florida.

Sunday 19th May:	leave London
Monday 20th May:	arrive in Florida - finish report find post office - send report
Tuesday 21st May:	get to conference - contact Professor Graham
Wednesday 22nd May:	give lecture - phone Geoffrey
Thursday 23rd May:	fly to London - plane arrives at 4 pm - drive straight home
Friday 24th May:	be at Institute

Now fill the gaps in the dialogue.

Geoffrey When will you leave?
Meg On Sunday.
Geoffrey The report is very important. When will you finish it?
Meg When I arrive in Florida. I ________ to you as soon as I find a post office.
Geoffrey What will you do when you get to the conference?
Meg I ________ Professor Graham.
Geoffrey When ________ your lecture?
Meg On Wednesday morning. ________ you as soon as I'm free.
Geoffrey Will you be at the Institute on Thursday?
Meg No, ________ at the Institute on Friday morning. ________ on Thursday and I'll drive straight home.

Miami Beach, Florida

Exercise 4

When you go to college or work tomorrow, what will you do? Write sentences like this:

When I arrive at work tomorrow, I'll have a cup of coffee.
I'll make some phone calls as soon as I finish my coffee.

LESSON 7

You Should Be More Ambitious

Have you got the qualities we are looking for?

Dr Geoffrey Walton is recruiting crew members for his *Save-The-Sea Expedition*. He is looking for the most exceptional candidates. They should be talented, intelligent and resourceful. They should have a strong spirit of adventure and they should be healthy and energetic. Do you fit this description? Are you sure? If your answer is 'yes', Dr Walton would like to hear from you.

The expedition, with its six crew members, will depart on 1st September. Your letter of application should reach us by 1st July. Write to:

Dr G Walton
The International Ocean Institute
32 Carlton Square Gardens
LONDON SW1 3NS

Suzy and her boyfriend, Dave, are having a drink in a local pub.

Dave Suzy, this isn't the advertisement you told me about, is it?
Suzy Yes, have you read it? You fit the description perfectly. You should apply.
Dave You're joking!
Suzy Dave! Be serious!
Dave You're not joking, are you, Suzy?
Suzy No, I'm not. You should make an application. You have all the right qualities. Jack Craig has applied and you're more intelligent than him.
Dave More intelligent! Are you certain about that?
Suzy Well, you've got better qualifications. You've got a university degree.
Dave Yes, and Jack's got practical experience. I'm not as experienced as him, am I?
Suzy Experience isn't as important as resourcefulness.
Dave I'm not as resourceful as him either.
Suzy You repaired my hairdryer last week. You were resourceful then.
Dave Yes, I took it to a qualified electrician and he repaired it.
Suzy Well, you're certainly more talented than Jack.
Dave I can't sail a yacht.
Suzy But you can play the piano.
Dave They don't need a piano player, Suzy. They need a sailor.
Suzy Oh, you're impossible, Dave. You should learn to sail a boat and you should apply to join the expedition. You should be more ambitious!
Dave And you should be more realistic.

Exercise 1

Answer the following questions.

1 Who should be more ambitious?
2 Who repaired Suzy's hairdryer?
3 Who should apply for the job?
4 Who is looking for exceptional candidates?
5 Who should be more realistic?
6 Who should learn to sail a boat?
7 What should reach the Institute by 1st July?

Exercise 2

What should they do? Match the sentences.

1 Meg wants to buy a new portable computer.
2 My radio doesn't work.
3 Dr Walton wants to read the applications, but Suzy and Meg are talking.
4 Dave can't repair Suzy's hairdryer.
5 Suzy bought a bikini yesterday, but it's too small for her.

a) He should go to his office.
b) You should get some new batteries for it.
c) He should take it to an electrician.
d) She should take it back to the shop.
e) She should borrow some money.

Underline all the examples of 'should' + verb above and complete the rule.

Rule: When we want to get someone's advice, we ask questions like:

What should I do?
When we give advice to someone, we can use:
You ________ + verb.

Exercise 3

Talk about Dave and Jack. Use the information below.

Qualities

Dave: intelligent – talented – relaxed – careful
Jack: experienced – resourceful – energetic – adventurous

Suzy Dr Walton should choose Dave.
Meg Are you sure? Why?
Suzy Dave's more intelligent than Jack?
Meg Yes, but Dave's not as experienced as Jack.

Think of someone who is well-known in your country. It can be a politician, an actor, a sportsman or woman, or a television personality. Work with your partner. Invent conversations like this:

You John McEnroe is faster than Stefan Edberg.
Your Partner Yes, but McEnroe is not as careful as Edberg.

See how many sentences like this you can make.

Exercise 4

Write a letter to a friend giving advice on how to learn a foreign language. Write sentences like this:

You should study for half an hour each day.
You should keep a list of new words.

Have you got a problem? Invent one if you haven't got one. Ask your partner to give you some advice. Find out your partner's problem and write down five pieces of advice to help solve his or her problem.

LESSON 8

Then I Worked in London

Exercise 1

Choose True or False. Then write the sentences from the text which give the answers.

1 Geoff wants someone who knows about photography.
2 Mrs Delporte got married, then left her job.
3 Meg doesn't want Mrs Delporte.
4 Robert and Jane are going to get married.
5 Robert is a radio operator.
6 Meg is sure that Charles is the right person.

Exercise 2

Study sentences (a) and (b) and complete the rule:

(a) First Peter met someone else. Then he left Maria.
Here the two events are given in the normal chronological sequence.

(b) Peter *left* me. He *had met* someone else.
Here the first chronological event is given in the second sentence.

Rule: If the first chronological event is given in the ________ sentence, then the verb form is the Past Perfect ('had' + past participle).

In the following pairs of sentences, which event happened first?

eg Peter left me. He had met someone else.
First Peter met someone else.

Jack saw Meg. He said 'hello'.
First Jack saw Meg.

1 Maria left her job. She got married.
2 Robert worked in London for a year. Next he got a job on an oil rig.
3 Robert and Jane quarrelled. Jane had gone out with someone else.
4 Charles was in video promotion. Then he was in property development.
5 Meg and Geoff chose Charles. They had interviewed him.
6 Meg and Geoff interviewed Maria Delporte. They didn't choose her.

Exercise 3

Reorder the phrases given below according to chronological sequence. Then use the new sequence to write a paragraph. Use 'next', 'then' and 'after that' to help link the sentences. Change the infinitive form verbs to Past Simple.

1 Anna – (leave school at 18) – (work as a dentist) – (get married to Sebastian) – (have three children) – (go to a College of Dentistry)

2 Jonathon – (apply for the post) – (resign from job as personnel assistant) – (see an advertisement for a personnel manager in the newspaper) – (leave college) – (take a job as a personnel assistant)

Exercise 4

Write down four sentences for four things you did in sequence yesterday. In pairs, tell each other what you did, as follows:

A: Tell B what you did first. (eg '*I went to the office.*')
B: Ask: '*What happened next?*'
A: Tell B what happened. (eg '*I spoke to my colleagues.*')
B: Ask: '*What happened next?*' etc.

Then change roles. B says what he did. A asks what happened.

LESSON 9

It's Bigger And Clearer

The team are all together in the Ocean Institute.

Meg Good morning, everyone. Thanks for coming. I want to explain what we're doing. Here's a map of our route.

Lisa Oh, Meg – haven't you got a better map? That one's awful! Here, take my map. It's bigger than that map, and clearer.

Meg Thanks. Now, I'll repeat our route in case you've forgotten. First we'll go from Plymouth to New York, then to the Caribbean, along the coast of South America, then Cape Horn.

Charles Why don't we go directly from England to Cape Horn? It's shorter than your route.

Meg Yes, it's shorter, but we want publicity, so it's America first. Then New Zealand, via the Pacific islands. After that Australia, Africa, Portugal, and home. Now, let's check the preparations. Lisa, you're preparing lists of interesting areas aren't you? . . . . .

Lisa Well, I'm preparing a list of the marine areas on our route. And I'm making a list of the food we want.

Jack I'm checking the condition of the boat. So far, there are no problems. Oh, have you got the spare keys for the cabins, Meg?

Charles I've got them. Otto gave them to me. He put new cupboards in the cabins. He says they're bigger than the old ones.

Meg He's very generous, isn't he?

Charles He's always been generous! By the way, Otto and I are contacting our business friends . . . . .

Meg Oh, yes. We've had offers of help from Global Tobacco, Rio Negro Metal, and National Petrol.

Lisa Who wants them? Rio Negro and NP pollute the sea! They're our enemies, aren't they!

Meg I know, Lisa. But they want us to advertise their names on the side of the boat. And they'll pay very well.

Yolanda I don't like it, but we have no choice. Just make the names really small!

Exercise 1

Answer the following questions.

1 Why does Lisa say 'Take my map'?
2 Why does Meg repeat their route?
3 Why does Meg want to go to America first?
4 What's Lisa doing to prepare for the trip?
5 And Jack?
6 And Charles?
7 Why doesn't Lisa want to advertise Rio Negro Metal and National Petrol?

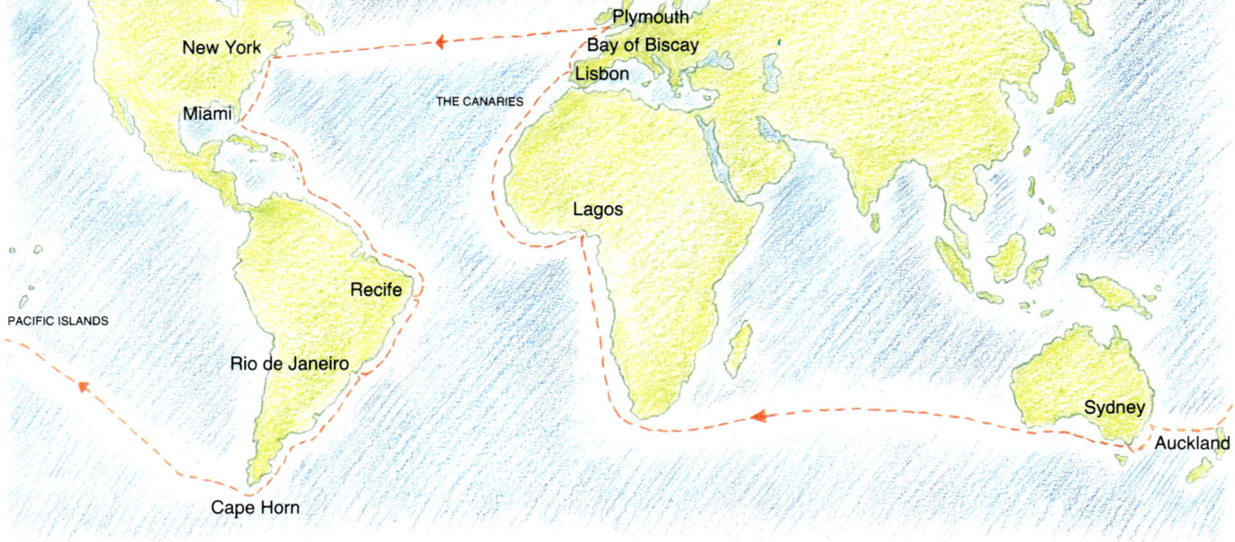

Exercise 2

'Bergman is very generous, *isn't he?*'

'Rio Negro Metal and National Petrol are our enemies, *aren't they?*'

'You're preparing lists of interesting areas, *aren't you?*'

To make a 'tag' after the affirmative form of the verb 'be' we use the negative interrogative of 'be', with the corresponding pronoun (I, you, he, she, it, we, they).
(Remember the exception: 'I'm your friend, *aren't I?*' not 'amn't I')

Finish the following sentences with the appropriate tag.

1 Lisa's angry about Rio Negro Metal and National Petrol, ________?
2 Charles is contacting his business friends, ________?
3 We're advertising their names, ________?
4 This is a bigger map, ________?
5 I'm seeing you tomorrow, ________?
6 Otto and Charles are contacting their business friends, ________?
7 You're going to America first, ________?
8 Meg is very efficient, ________?

Exercise 3

Example:

Jack: *I'm checking* the condition of the boat.

Notice that the Present Continous is sometimes used to indicate things which are going on, but not necessarily at the moment of speaking.

Practise the dialogue with a partner. Use the following phrases to help you. Take turns to be A and B. (Remember to change the verb form.)

A: What are you doing these days?
B: (1) I'm learning to drive. What about you?
A: Nothing much. (2) I'm working in a bank.
B: Oh, (2) I'm working in a bank too.

(1) learn French/Italian/Arabic/Spanish; build a boat; paint my house

(2) study for my exams; work in an office; go to evening classes

Exercise 4

Now write a paragraph saying what you are doing these days, whether it is easy or difficult, and whether or not you like it.

LESSON 10

I've Been Looking for a New Position

Meg receives a letter from Charles.

Hasdene,
Culverton Avenue
Richmond W11 3EK

July 19th

Dear Meg,

I'm very sorry to tell you that I cannot be a member of your expedition. As you know, I have been looking for a new position. Now a friend has offered me an interesting job as a director of Stateside Tour Agencies, working in London and New York.

I am afraid that I cannot refuse this offer. I am very sorry to disappoint you. I shall support your expedition in every way, and I wish you good luck.

Yours sincerely,

Charles Durberville

Charles Durberville

PS See you in New York!

Three days later, Meg and Geoffrey receive another letter.

Dear Dr Brooke,

I am writing to apply for a place on your voyage around the world. I understand that Mr Charles Durberville has withdrawn.

I am 35 years old, and worked for eleven years as Head Forester at Bagshot Estates, in charge of 5000 hectares of forest. Two years ago I was made redundant and received a large redundancy payment. Since then, I have been working as a forestry consultant. I now intend to do something different. I have been sailing small boats for the past five years.

I can meet you at any time next week to discuss matters.

Yours sincerely,

Howard Ellway

Howard Ellway

The group meets Howard the following week.
Then Meg writes to Jack.

Jack,

A brief note. Geoff and I offered the place to Howard and he accepted. You and Lisa don't like him, I know. He *is* a show-off, but he seems efficient. He's only been sailing for a couple of years, but he'll be useful. We must take him. I haven't been sleeping for days – I haven't been eating properly either. I've been worrying about this last place. There's no one else!

Meg

Exercise 1

Answer the following questions.

1 Why can't Charles join the expedition?
2 Which countries is Charles going to work in?
3 What does Howard Ellway want to do?
4 What did he do for more than ten years?
5 Did Geoff and Meg offer the job to Howard?
6 Why doesn't Jack like Howard?

Exercise 2

'Since then, *I've been working* as a forestry consultant.'

The above verb form is called the Present Perfect Continuous. It consists of: 'have/has' + 'been' + verb+'ing'.
(In spoken language '*have*' = '*ve*' and '*has*' = ''*s*', except with short answer forms, eg *Yes, I have*, not *Yes, I've.*)

Complete the following table. Use the full forms of 'have':

I have been working
You have ____ ____
He has ____ ____
She ____ ____ ____
It ____ ____ ____

We ____ ____ ____
They ____ ____ ____
John ____ ____ ____
Meg and Lisa ____ ____ ____
The machine ____ ____ ____

Exercise 3

The Present Perfect Continuous is used to show that an action started in the past, and (a) is still continuing:
eg *I've been waiting a long time* (I'm still waiting at this moment)
or (b) is not finished:
eg *I've been taking Arabic lessons* (I'm not taking one at this moment, but I am going to continue.)

Find four more examples of this verb form in Lesson 10.

Study the dialogue. In pairs, make up similar dialogues. Take turns to be A and B. Use the phrases below to help you. (Remember to use the correct form of the verb.)

A: What on earth have you been doing?
B: I've been (1) working in the garden.
A: (1) Working in the garden! Well, I've been waiting (2) for twenty minutes!
B: Oh dear, (2) twenty minutes! I *am* sorry!

(1) reading the paper; talking to a friend; watching television; writing a letter

(2) for a quarter of an hour; since midday; since six o'clock; for half an hour

Exercise 4

Write a short paragraph about yourself describing the activities that you have, or have not been doing recently.

LESSON 11

If There's No Wind . . .

Geoffrey, Jack, Meg and Lisa are looking at the boat.

Jack Well, here she is! The *Ocean Investigator*.
Lisa That's an odd name. A bit technical. If we call her the *Ocean Investigator*, people will think we're trying to discover new countries! Meg, you like the *Good Hope*, don't you?
Meg I'm not sure. People will think we're a religious group if we call her the *Good Hope*.
Jack So what do you suggest, Meg?
Meg I like the *Ocean Explorer*.
Geoff Good! That's that! Now, where are the sails?
Jack In the locker.
Lisa What shall we do if there's no wind?
Jack If there's no wind, we'll use the engine. If we try to get around using only the sails, we'll take forever. Come on, let's go below.
Meg This cabin's mine, this is yours Lisa, and that's yours Yolanda.
Lisa Oh, they're really beautiful! This is going to be a holiday! But mine's bigger than yours.
Meg Not really. It's longer but it's narrower, so it's about the same size.
Lisa And these three cabins here are for Jack, Howard, and Robert.
Jack And my cabin's the biggest.
Lisa Howard won't like that.
Meg But Jack keeps a lot of equipment, doesn't he? That's why his is the biggest.
Lisa And Howard's mouth is the biggest!
Meg Lisa, if you say things like that, this voyage will be a disaster! But at least you like Robert, don't you?
Lisa Yes. And perhaps Howard isn't so bad!

Exercise 1

Choose True or False. Then write the sentences which give the answers.

1 Lisa likes the name *Ocean Investigator*.
2 Geoff can see the sails.
3 Lisa likes the cabins.
4 Howard has got the biggest cabin.
5 Lisa thinks that Howard talks too much.
6 Meg decides to call the boat the *Good Hope*.

Exercise 2

'If you talk like that, this voyage will be a disaster!'

This sentence is in two parts or *clauses*. The clause with 'If' states the condition. The other clause states what will happen if the condition happens. Complete the rule.

Rule: In a sentence talking about a simple condition in the future, the verb in the 'If' clause is in the ________ Tense.
The other clause contains 'shall/ will' + verb.
(Remember 'shall' usually with 'I' and 'we';
'will' with others.
'will not' in speech usually becomes 'won't')

Find the other examples of sentences with 'if' in the dialogue.

Finish the sentences in Column 1 by choosing from Column 2.

1

1 Howard will be unhappy . . . . .
2 They'll use the engine . . . . .
3 The journey will take forever . . . . .
4 Robert won't see his girlfriend . . . . .
5 The voyage will be a disaster . . . . .

2

a) if he goes on the trip.
b) if Lisa is rude about Howard.
c) if Jack has the biggest cabin.
d) if there is no wind.
e) if they never use the engine.

Exercise 3

Pat and Chris are not very good friends. They use a lot of 'if's'! Read the dialogue, and then in pairs make similar dialogues using the phrases given. Take turns to be Pat and Chris.

Pat If you go to town tomorrow, will you buy me (1) a blank video tape?
Chris Sure – and if I buy you the tape, will you lend me your (2) video magazine?
Pat OK! But if you forget the tape, I won't lend it.
Chris Don't worry! If you give me the money for the tape now, I won't forget it!
Pat But I'm broke!

(1) the latest *Sky* magazine; the *Radio Times*; some audio cassettes; four C60 batteries for my radio

(2) transistor radio; new record; torch; bicycle; dictionary

Exercise 4

Think of three places that you know. Write a paragraph comparing them. Use '. . . . . er (than)' and 'the . . . . . est'.Here is the beginning of an example:

I'm going to write about Newcastle, Birmingham and Brighton. I have been to all of them, so I know them well. Birmingham is the biggest. Newcastle is bigger than Brighton. All three are full of traffic and so they are very noisy, but Birmingham is the noisiest. Birmingham is more expensive than Newcastle, and Brighton is more expensive than Birmingham. . . . .

Brighton Pier

LESSON 12

I Am Totally Rejected

Exercise 1

Choose True or False. Then write the sentences from the text which give the answers.

1 Rob is the first to arrive.
2 Jane wants Rob to go.
3 Rob decides to stay.
4 Yolanda is taking eight cameras.
5 There is some alcohol on the boat.
6 The team members quarrel sometimes.

Exercise 2

Study the two sentences, and complete the rule.

I *am rejected*. My letters *are returned*.

Rule: The Present Simple Passive form, consists of *two* parts:
i) the Present of the verb 'be' (eg 'am')
ii) the ________ participle (eg 'rejected')

Complete the table with the Present Simple Passive of 'to reject'.

I am rejected	We _____ _____
You are _____	You _____ _____
He is _____	They _____ _____
She is _____	
It _____ _____	

Complete the following sentences, using the Present Simple Passive form of the verb 'speak'.

Example: . . . . . by most people in Quebec.

French is spoken by most people in Quebec.

1 ________ by everyone in New Zealand.
2 ________ in Spain, and many South American countries.
3 ________ in Italy.
4 ________ in Portugal and Brazil.
5 ________ in Germany and Austria.
6 ________ in Sweden.
7 ________ in Greece.

Exercise 3

Robert doesn't want to stay, *does he?*

The first part of the sentence has a negative with 'doesn't/don't'. The last part has the interrogative with 'does/do'. Tag questions like this are used if the speaker expects the answer 'No'.

Change the following sentences into questions that expect the answer 'No'.

Example:

You quarrel too much.
You don't quarrel too much, do you?

1 Your brother drinks a lot of beer.
2 Aunt Mary wants to visit us tomorrow.
3 They like American television programmes.
4 This book costs a lot of money.
5 Yolanda takes photographs all the time.

Exercise 4

Study the conversation below, then make similar conversations, using the phrases. Remember to change 'these' to 'this' if necessary.

A: You don't want another (1) cake, do you?
B: Yes, I do. You don't like these cakes, do you?
A: No, I don't. They're too (2) sweet.
B: Why don't you try these (3) sandwiches instead?
A: Thanks. I will.

(1) biscuit; apple; pear; orange
(2) hard; sour
(3) sausages; grapes; peaches; bananas

Exercise 5

Imagine you are writing for an English magazine. Write a description of wine making, using the information below. Begin by putting the information in the correct order and then write the description, using sequence words to show the order.

Sequence words: first, next, then, after that, finally
the bottles – are distributed
the grape juice – is left to ferment
the wine – is bottled
the grapes – are picked – are put into containers – are crushed

LESSON 13

It's Going to Be My Last Chance

At sea in the Atlantic, Howard, Yolanda and Robert discuss what they are going to do in New York. Yolanda has a surprise for Robert.

Howard Well, Yolanda, what are you going to do when you get to New York?
Yolanda Visit Harvey's Deli.
Howard Why?
Yolanda Because, Howard, they have the most delicious salt beef sandwiches in the world.
Robert Salt beef sandwiches?
Yolanda Sure. You like salt beef sandwiches, don't you?
Robert Well, maybe.
Howard You went to Bloom's when you were in London, didn't you, Yolanda?
Robert Bloom's?
Yolanda Yeah. They're famous for salt beef sandwiches and Jewish food. They're in the East End of London.
Robert Oh, I see. And you tried their salt beef sandwiches, didn't you?
Yolanda Sure I did. Bloom's are the finest in London. But Harvey's are the most fantastic in the world!
Robert Scotland has got good beef too – and fish!
Howard And porridge!
Robert Lots of Scots don't eat porridge, Howard.
Howard I'm just teasing, Rob. Lots of Englishmen don't eat roast beef and Yorkshire pudding, either. Anyway, Rob, what are you going to do in New York?
Robert Don't know. What do you suggest?
Yolanda You come along with me, baby. You're going to have the most exciting time of your life!
Howard Hey, Rob, that's an offer you can't refuse!
Robert Maybe. But I don't like salt beef sandwiches.

Exercise 1

Answer the following questions.

1 Why is Yolanda going to visit Harvey's Deli?
2 Where can you obtain the best salt beef sandwiches in London?
3 In which country do some people eat porridge?
4 What is Yolanda going to give Rob in New York?
5 Why won't Bob enjoy it?

Exercise 2

Complete the following sequence:

fine → finer → ________
delicious → more delicious → ________ ________
fantastic → more fantastic → ________ ________

Make the comparative and superlative forms of the following adjectives and then use four of them in sentences of your own.

tall	fascinating
athletic	disappointing
versatile	short
difficult	big
small	

Exercise 3

In the dialogue, two questions tags are used:
You like salt beef sandwiches, *don't you?*
You went to Bloom's when you were in London, *didn't you?*

Rule:
When we use an affirmative statement, we use a negative question tag. In the ________ Tense we use 'don't' with all persons, except *he, she, it*. With them we use 'doesn't'.

Example:

She likes salt beef sandwiches, ________ she?
He likes salt beef sandwiches, *doesn't* ________?

We use ________ for all persons with the Past Tense.

Example:

He lived in Scotland, ________ he?
She lived in England, *didn't* ________?

Now complete these sentences with appropriate tags.

1 They borrowed a yacht, ________?
2 Charles went to New York, ________?
3 Lisa learnt to cook Indian food, ________?
4 Yolanda takes photographs, ________?
5 We finished *Formula 1* last year, ________?

Exercise 4

A's Diary

MONDAY	Finish Paris seminar paper
TUESDAY	Flight BA633 to Paris
WEDNESDAY	All day in Paris
THURSDAY	Free
FRIDAY	Meeting district manager

B's Diary

MONDAY	Play rehearsal
TUESDAY	Evening class
WEDNESDAY	Meeting in London
THURSDAY	Visit to headquarters
FRIDAY	Free

Two friends are trying to arrange to see each other next week. They go through their diaries. Practise the dialogue with a partner.

A: What are you doing on Monday?
B: I'm going to a play rehearsal. And you?
A: I'm finishing my Paris seminar paper. So Monday's out.
B: Yes. What about Tuesday? I'm going to evening class.
A: And I'm going to Paris and I'm there on Wednesday.
B: So, that's Tuesday and Wednesday out.
A: What about Thursday? I'm free then.
B: No, I'm visiting headquarters all day. But I'm free on Friday.
A: That's no good for me. I'm meeting the district manager.
B: Oh, well, let's leave our meeting till next month.
A: Yes, we'll have to.

Now with a partner, write your diaries for next week. Try to arrange a meeting in your free time with each other.

LESSON 14

If You Contact Him, He'll Help You

At the Ocean Institute, Geoffrey Walton is sending a radio message to Meg.

Geoff Suzy, can you arrange to get this message off today some time?
Suzy Yes, I'm going down to International Sea Radio later. I'll deliver it then. They'll transmit it for us at 2100 hours GMT.
Geoff That's a bit late, isn't it?
Suzy No, Rob is expecting us to send radio messages then. We can't just call him at any time, you know. Anyway, if I leave in half an hour, I'll be there in plenty of time.

From: Director, Geoffrey Walton
To: Expedition Leader, Meg Brooke
Re: Contacts

I've sent telexes to some of our contacts around the world. So far, I've received replies from the USA, Jamaica, New Zealand and Australia. I'm waiting for replies from Argentina, Chile, Nigeria, and Portugal.

If you call Chuck Wagner at UBC in New York, he'll arrange media contacts for publicity. In Jamaica, Rodney Squires will help if you need supplies. If you stop in Recife on your way south, contact Carlos Couto. He'll introduce to you the local oceanographic survey team. Julio O'Brien in Buenos Aires will help you if you want advice on the voyage round Cape Horn. In New Zealand, get in touch with Koro Hohepa if you want to meet the fisheries research people. In Australia, contact Betty Singleton. She'll introduce you to the most important media people.

I'm faxing addresses, telex numbers and other details to New York tomorrow. Meanwhile, more offers of sponsorship are coming in. All the best to you all.

Geoffrey

Exercise 1

Complete the following table with information from the texts.

Place	Person	What he or she will do
New York		
	Rodney Squires	
		introduce you to the oceanographic survey team
Buenos Aires		
	Koro Hohepa	
		introduce you to media people

Exercise 2

In Lesson 11, you were introduced to this conditional pattern:

'If' clause	**Other clause**
'If' + Present Tense	'will' + verb

Example:

If you call Chuck Wagner, he'll arrange media contacts.

In this lesson, there is another kind of conditional pattern:

'If' clause	**Other clause**
'If' + Present Tense	verb

Example:

If you stop in Recife, contact Carlos Couto.

Find an example of each sentence in Geoff's message.
Match the A and B parts of the sentences below.

A

1 If you want a cheap lunch,
2 If you go to San Antonio,
3 If you like Mexican cooking,
4 If you want a good exchange rate,
5 If you want to get some souvenirs,
6 If you want to phone home,

B

a) wait till after six o'clock.
b) avoid the bureau de change.
c) visit the Alamo.
d) try Casa Pepe.
e) pick up a sandwich at Schilo's Deli.
f) go to the Hippie Market on Sunday.

Exercise 3

Practise the dialogue with a partner. Take turns at being A and B.

A: What are you doing?
B: I'm going (1) to the supermarket.
A: It's a bit (2) late, isn't it? It's closed now.
B: No, I don't think so. (3) Anyway, if I leave now, I'll be in time.
A: OK, but I hope you're right.

(1) for a walk; for a run; to the pub; to catch the London coach
*

(2) cold, isn't it? The weather's wintry today; early, isn't it? It doesn't open till 6; late, isn't it? It leaves at half past.
*

(3) Anyway, if I move quickly, I'll keep warm; Anyway, if I take my time, it will be open; Anyway, if I hurry, I'll catch it.
*

* Use your own information.

Exercise 4

A visitor has asked you for advice on places to visit in your country or town. List places like this:

Places	Things to see there

Then write six sentences, following the two patterns in Exercise 2.

Examples:

If you go to Paris, visit the Musée d'Orsay.
If you go to the Musée d'Orsay, you'll be impressed.

LESSON 15

Do You Think They're Quarrelling?

At the Ocean Institute, Suzy reports a radio message from Meg to Geoffrey.

Geoff Hello, Suzy. Are there any messages?
Suzy Yes, there's another one from Meg.
Geoff What's it about?
Suzy Something about the crew.
Geoff Oh, no! Do you think she's got problems?
Suzy I don't know. She didn't actually say.
Geoff Do you think they're quarrelling?
Suzy No, I don't think so.
Geoff Why not?
Suzy Meg always says what she thinks.
Geoff Hmm. Was there anything else?
Suzy Yes, she asked if Chuck Wagner was expecting them.
Geoff Yes, I've already telexed him and I mentioned it in my last message. Was there anything else?
Suzy Yes, she asked if you could send more money for supplies.
Geoff Did she say how much?
Suzy Yes. Five thousand dollars.
Geoff Five thousand dollars! Are you sure?
Suzy Yes, I think so. She said they need more food and equipment.
Geoff OK. I'll make arrangements tomorrow.
Suzy Alright. Is that all for now?
Geoff Yes. Oh, just one thing. Suzy. Do you think they're a happy crew?
Suzy I don't know. It's a long, tough voyage. And they haven't sailed together before.
Geoff Suzy, you're a real pessimist, aren't you? Now, how about a cup of coffee?

Exercise 1

Complete the following with 'Yes', 'Uncertain' or 'No'.

	Yes	Uncertain	No
1 There is trouble with the crew.			
2 Suzy thinks they are quarrelling.			
3 Meg says what she thinks.			
4 They're short of money.			
5 Geoff is going to telex Chuck Wagner.			
6 They're a happy crew.			

Exercise 2

Read the dialogue again and complete the answers to the question.

Do you think . . . . .?

Yes, I think _________.

No, I _________ so.

No, I don't _________.

When we give an answer like the ones above, we can also give a reason, eg

A: Do you think Meg will say nothing?
B: No, I don't think so. *Meg always says what she thinks.*

Now write the answers to the following questions and add an appropriate reason from the sentences given.

1 Do you think it's going to rain?
No, I _________.
2 Do you think it's going to be hot tomorrow?
Yes, I _________.
3 Do you think the crew are quarrelling?
No, I _________.
4 Do you think they will reach New York safely?
Yes, I _________.
5 Do you think they will be successful?
Yes, I _________.
6 Does Suzy think they will be successful?
No, she _________.

Reasons

a) They're a very strong team.
b) Today was very warm.
c) Meg didn't say anything about it.
d) She thinks it's a long, tough voyage.
e) They have a good boat.
f) There are no clouds in the sky.

Exercise 3

Suzy reports these questions to Geoff.

Is Chuck Wagner expecting us?
Can you send us more money for supplies?

Find the sentences in which she reports them. Note the changes which occur.

Is becomes _________.
Can becomes _________.

The word order changes:

Direct Speech: *Is* X coming?
Indirect Speech: She asked if X *was* coming.

Report these questions.

1 Can Meg come to the party? Lisa asked . . . . .
2 Is Jack coming to the party? Rob asked . . . . .
3 Can I pay by credit card? Yolanda asked . . . . .
4 Are the crew happy? Geoff asked . . . . .
5 Can Meg have more money? Suzy asked . . . . .
6 Is the ship in New York? Geoff asked . . . . .

Exercise 4

List three things you want to ask your partner, eg *Do you think X is good for you?* Ask and answer the questions with 'Yes/No' answers (as in Exercise 2) and give a reason.

LESSON 16

We May Not Survive

Exercise 1

Choose True or False. Then write the sentences from the text which give the answers.

1 The weather in the south is better than the weather in the north.
2 Jack is worried about the storm.
3 There are always storms in the mid-Atlantic.
4 Jack is happy with Howard.
5 It is not the worst storm in Jack's life.
6 In the USA there is no duty on cut diamonds.
7 The US customs men are going to watch the boat carefully.

Exercise 2

Study the examples:

'*You may go.*' Here 'may' is used to give permission.

'*There may be more.*' (= Perhaps there are more.)

'*We may not survive this.*' (= Perhaps we will not survive this.) Here 'may' is used to show that the speaker is not certain.

Find other examples of 'may' in the text.

Change the following sentences, using 'may'.

1 Perhaps there are more packets of diamonds on the boat.
2 Perhaps the wind will be too strong soon.
3 Perhaps the team will not survive this storm.
4 Perhaps the smugglers will stop you at sea.
5 Perhaps Howard wants to go to bed.
6 Perhaps Jack doesn't like Howard.
7 Perhaps the team will not raise enough money on the trip.
8 Perhaps Yolanda will not take photographs of the storm.

Exercise 3

Study the dialogue below, and, in pairs, make similar dialogues, with the necessary changes. Take turns to be A and B.

A: What are you going to do this evening?
B: I'm not sure. I may (1) write some letters to old friends.
A: If you finish by (2) nine, why don't we (3) meet at the pub?
B: Well, OK. I may be late. And the pub isn't as cheap as it was last year.
A: I know. And it isn't as (4) cheerful either. But it's better than nothing!
B: That's for sure!

(1) make telephone calls to all my family; work late at the office; do some homework (Then make up your own ideas.)

(2) eight; eight-thirty (Make up your own time.)

(3) have a drink at the café; go to the fair; go to the late-night disco (Then make up your own ideas.)

(4) interesting; entertaining; lively

Exercise 4

Imagine you are writing a letter to an old friend. Tell your friend about the things you are going to do, and the things you may do.

LESSON 17

He Told Me to Stop Wasting Time

Lisa is preparing a meal. Robert joins her in the ship's galley.

Lisa I still can't believe it. A fortune in diamonds on our yacht and we didn't know! It's incredible! Do you think we'll get a reward?
Robert I don't think so.
Lisa Yes, but we found the diamonds . . .
Robert Yeah, they'll probably put us in gaol for smuggling.
Lisa Are you all right, Rob?
Robert Yes. Why?
Lisa Well, you look a bit . . . well, I don't know . . . you look a bit annoyed.
Robert Yes, you're right. I've just had an argument with Howard.
Lisa Goodness! What about?
Robert Oh, nothing important.
Lisa Come on, Rob, you can tell me.
Robert No, it's too complicated to explain.
Lisa Howard's really upset you. Come on, tell me what he said.
Robert Well, we were clearing up all that mess on the deck and he tried to tell me what to do.
Lisa What do you mean?
Robert First he told me to get a mop and bucket and wash the deck. Then after that he told me to move some boxes and stack them in a corner.
Lisa And did you?
Robert No, certainly not. They were too heavy to lift so I went back into the radio room.
Lisa Then what happened?
Robert He shouted at me and told me to stop wasting time and do some real work for a change.
Lisa What a nerve! What did you say?
Robert I didn't say anything, but Yolanda heard him and she told him to leave me alone.
Lisa I bet he didn't like that.
Robert No, he didn't. He told her to mind her own business. She was furious. She went straight out and called Meg.
Lisa What did Meg say?
Robert She asked Howard to explain the problem and he told her I was too lazy to do any work.
Lisa That's awful! What did Meg say about that?
Robert She told us not to argue and she told Howard to go and stack his own boxes.
Lisa I should think so too. And what did she say to you?
Robert She told me not to worry and have a cup of tea. So here I am! Any tea?
Lisa Right away . . . and forget about the argument. I'm sure it was only a storm in a teacup!

Exercise 1

Read the dialogue and put the sentences in the right order:

a) Meg told Howard and Rob not to argue. ____
b) The crew didn't know about the diamonds. ____
c) Howard told Rob to move some boxes. ____
d) Yolanda called Meg. ____
e) Rob joined Lisa in the ship's galley. __1__
f) Howard went back to the radio room. ____
g) Lisa made Rob a cup of tea. ____
h) Howard shouted at Rob. ____
i) Rob told Lisa about his argument with Howard. ____
j) Howard explained the problem to Meg. ____

Exercise 2

Study these sentences.

'Get a mop and bucket.'
Howard told Rob to get a mop and bucket.

'Don't argue!'
Meg told Rob and Howard not to argue.

Who gave these orders? Who did they give them to? Write sentences as in the example.

1 'Leave him alone!'

____

2 'Don't argue!'

____

3 'Move some boxes.'

____

4 'Mind your own business.'

____

5 'Go and stack your own boxes.'

____

6 'Don't worry!'

____

Exercise 3

Study these sentences.

Rob's argument with Howard is *too complicated to explain.*
The boxes were *too heavy to lift.*

Now choose one word from Box 1 and one word from Box 2 and complete the sentences.

Box 1

heavy hot expensive complicated long full tasteless

Box 2

close read explain buy lift drink eat

1 The diamonds are ____________________.
2 Howard's cooking is ____________________.
3 Meg's report is ____________________.
4 Lisa's tea is ____________________.
5 Rob's suitcase is ____________________.

Exercise 4

Think about things that people told you to do this week. Write five sentences, like this:

My doctor told me to take these tablets twice a day for five days.

Think about instructions that other people were given this week. Write five sentences, like this:

My cousin told her husband to do the shopping.

LESSON 18

What Will Happen Next?

Meg is writing an entry in her personal log.

18th September

Personal Log

This is the 14th day of our voyage and all of the crew are tired. They've worked very hard and it's not surprising that some of them have begun to quarrel. Yesterday Howard nearly started an unpleasant argument with Rob, but fortunately they've both calmed down and things are almost back to normal.

I'll be very glad when we reach the USA because up to now it hasn't exactly been smooth sailing. First we had the trouble of finding a substitute for Charles Durberville. Then we had that freak storm, followed by the discovery of the diamonds. What will happen next? Well, who knows? I do know that there will be real trouble if Howard doesn't change his attitude towards the rest of the crew. He's been making life on board ship very difficult.

In the meantime there are more urgent matters. There will be a lot to do when we arrive in New York. The US customs officials will inspect the boat and they'll ask a lot of questions, too. I'll phone Geoffrey as soon as the customs officials complete their enquiry and I'll tell him about the diamonds.

There are other things to do as well. Before we arrive, Howard and Yolanda will check our general supplies. Then, as soon as they can, Jack and Rob will buy the equipment we need and Lisa will take care of food supplies: she'll order any other important items that we need for the next stage of the journey.

Exercise 1

Read Meg's log and answer the following questions.

1 When will Meg be very glad?
2 What will happen if Howard doesn't change his attitude?
3 When will there be a lot to do?
4 What will the US customs officials do?
5 When will Meg phone Geoffrey?
6 What will she tell him?
7 What will Howard and Yolanda do before they arrive in New York?
8 When will Jack and Rob buy the equipment they need?

Exercise 2

Join the sentences with 'as soon as'.

Example:

Meg has enough money. Meg will buy a computer.
Meg will buy a computer as soon as she has enough money.

1 Lisa has time. Lisa will finish her research paper.

____

2 The expedition is over. Howard is going to look for a new job.

____

3 The yacht arrives in New York. US customs officials will contact Meg.

____

4 Jack is free. Jack will visit his friends.

____

5 Yolanda gets some film. Yolanda will take more photographs.

____

6 Rob finds a guide. Rob will go sightseeing.

____

Rule: Verbs that come after 'as soon as' and refer to future time are in the Simple Present Tense.

Exercise 3

Complete the sentences with 'some' or 'all'.

Example:

Jack had a box of chocolates and Lisa ate *some* of them. She ate six altogether.
Yolanda had three packets of crisps. Today she hasn't got any. Howard ate *all* of them.

1 There was one packet of biscuits. Rob ate the whole packet. He ate ________ of the biscuits.
2 There were six eggs in the larder yesterday. Now there are only three. Rob ate ________ of the eggs.
3 Yesterday there were five cans of beer left in the fridge. Today there are two cans in the fridge. Jack drank ________ of them.
4 There were four oranges in the fruit bowl today. Yesterday there were seven. Lisa ate ________ of them.
5 There were four sandwiches on the table at lunch time. Now there are no sandwiches. Howard ate ________ of them.

Exercise 4

Write a list of five things that you will do as soon as you finish your English class today. Write sentences like this:

As soon as I finish my English class, I'll have a cup of coffee.

What will you do as soon as you have enough money? Write down five ideas and then compare your list with your partner's. Write sentences like this:

As soon as I have enough money, I'll go on a world cruise.

LESSON 19

If I Were You, I'd Relax

Otto Bergman and Charles Durberville are having a telephone conversation.

Bergman . . . so the *Ocean Explorer* will arrive as scheduled on Friday. You will simply collect the shipment and deliver it.
Durberville But what if the crew have discovered the diamonds?
Bergman You're such a pessimist, Charles. If I were you I'd relax.
Durberville OK. What's the plan? What have I got to do?
Bergman First, you'll make contact with the crew. You'll pay a surprise visit to the boat. If I were you I'd take some champagne. . . . .
Durberville And some caviar!
Bergman Right. Throw a little celebration party. That way you'll break the ice and gain their confidence. They'll tell you if anything unusual has happened. Then invite all of them to the party at the Yacht Club. They'll appreciate that.
Durberville Good. So somebody will collect the diamonds when the crew are at the party.
Bergman No. You'll collect them a few days later – just before the yacht leaves New York. Cornelius will go with you.

Durberville Don't you trust me, Otto?
Bergman Of course, my dear Charles, but you'll need help.
Durberville You're very considerate!
Bergman Now, you know where to look, don't you?
Durberville In the black girl's cabin.
Bergman That's right. You'll put some of the diamonds in your bag and Cornelius will bring the rest. If I were you, I'd move quickly after that.
Durberville We'll make an excuse and leave the boat.
Bergman Fine. Then you'll leave the port together in the same car, but you'll drive straight to the Hadleigh motel.
Durberville The Hadleigh. OK.
Bergman They'll give you the key to room 39. A man will be there. He'll pay you the money. Give him the diamonds.
Durberville Yes, but what if . . . . . ?
Bergman Just take the money and go.
Durberville Who'll pay me? Will he be on time? What if . . . . . ?
Bergman If I were you, I wouldn't ask any more questions.

Exercise 1

Choose True or False. Then write the sentences from the text that give the answers.

1 The *Ocean Explorer* will arrive on Saturday.
2 Charles is worried.
3 Charles will visit the yacht and invite the crew to a party.
4 Somebody will collect the diamonds when the crew are at the Yacht Club party.
5 Otto Bergman will help Charles to collect the diamonds.
6 Charles will put all of the diamonds in his bag.
7 Charles and Cornelius will travel together in the same car.

Exercise 2

Otto Bergman gives Charles four pieces of advice. What does he say?
Read the dialogue and complete the sentences.

1 If I were you, ________ quickly.
2 If I were you, ________ some champagne.
3 If I were you, ________ any more questions.
4 If I were you, ________.

These people have all got problems. Give them advice.

Example:
'I can't find my car.' (telephone)
If I were you, I'd telephone the police.

1 'I've got a bad cough.' (stop smoking)
____

2 'I feel very tired.' (go)
____

3 'Someone has stolen my suitcase.' (call)
____

4 'I've got a headache.' (take)
____

Rule: We use the second conditional to ask for advice in sentences like this:

'*What would you do, if you were me?*' To give advice, we can say: 'If I ________ you, I would + verb.'

In second conditional sentences with 'be', we generally use 'were' after 'If'.
Here are some more examples:

If Jack were here, we'd have a great time.
You'd feel more comfortable, if you were at home.

Exercise 3

Charles is worried and he's asking Otto a lot of questions. Read what he's worried about and ask his questions.

Example:
The crew may suspect me.
What if the crew suspect me?
The crew may not invite me on board the yacht.
What if the crew don't invite me on board the yacht?

1 The police may suspect me.
____

2 They may not give me the key to room 39.
____

3 I may be late for the appointment.
____

4 The man at the Hadleigh Motel may be an imposter.
____

5 The man may not give me the money.
____

Exercise 4

Write down five problems you or your friends have got. If you haven't got any problems, invent some.
Exchange lists with your partner and, after studying his or her problems, write a letter suggesting some solutions. Begin like this:

'I've considered your problems very carefully.
If I were you . . . . .'

Give reasons for each of the solutions you suggest.

LESSON 20

If You Don't Go, She Might Eat You

Exercise 1

Choose True or False. Then write the sentences from the text that give the answers.

1 The US customs are watching them carefully.
2 Rob thinks New York is wonderful.
3 Yolanda wants to show Rob New York.
4 Rob wants to pay for the evening.
5 Rob and Yolanda enjoy themselves.

Exercise 2

'*I might stay on board tonight.*' (= Perhaps I shall stay on board tonight.)

'might' is used to show the speaker is not certain. (The difference of certainty between 'may' and 'might' is very small – 'may' is more formal.)

Rewrite the following sentences using 'might'.

1 Perhaps I'll stay on board.
2 Perhaps I won't go out.
3 Perhaps we'll have a drink first.
4 Perhaps they'll go home late.
5 Perhaps I'm not progressive.
6 Perhaps I'll start saving next month.
7 Perhaps the new government will solve our problems.
8 Perhaps I'll sell my car, and buy a bicycle.

Exercise 3

Study the dialogue, then in pairs make similar dialogues. Take turns to be A and B, and make sure that the dialogue makes sense.

A: Next month I might start (1) to play a musical instrument.
B: Good idea. And I might (1) take cooking lessons.
A: Right. I might (2) play the piano.
B: And I might (2) try vegetarian cooking.

(1) to play a sport; to take regular exercise; to make my own clothes

(2) make a hat; make a skirt; knit a pair of socks; go swimming; go jogging; go for an early-morning walk; play rugby; play tennis; play squash (make up your own activities)

Exercise 4

'*It looks suspicious!*'
'*I think New York looks a bit frightening.*'
'*That picture looks very frightening.*'

Make sentences with 'look(s)' and an adjective (eg *suspicious, frightening*) about the team (Meg, Jack, Yolanda, Robert, Howard and Lisa).
You can use these adjectives: happy, sad, clever, silly, rich, poor, funny, serious, generous, mean.
Use 'a bit' or 'very' if you want to.

Make similar sentences about people or places that you know.

New York, Manhattan

LESSON 21

Someone Had Hidden It There

The expedition has arrived in New York, where a customs officer comes aboard the yacht to interview Meg and Yolanda.

Officer Where were you, ma'am?
Yolanda In the cabin. We went there after the storm had started. It was too dangerous to stay on deck.
Officer When did you discover the diamonds?
Yolanda After my camera box had crashed against the cupboard. A big wave hit us and the camera box slammed against the cupboard, breaking the wooden panels.
Officer What happened next?
Yolanda We found some packets behind the panels.
Meg Obviously, someone had put them there before we sailed.
Yolanda We opened the packets and discovered the diamonds. Obviously, someone wanted us to smuggle them into the States. Our expedition is a perfect cover for a smuggling operation. And, as you know, there's very high duty on cut diamonds.
Officer True. How many diamonds did you find?
Yolanda Well, in my cabin there were several packets. But we didn't search for any more. We had survived the storm, and there was a lot to do on deck. The boat was a mess.
Meg Yes, after we had repaired some damage to the boat, our radio operator, Rob, contacted the Coast Guard about our discovery.
Officer So, you were sailing on a ship loaded with diamonds.
Yolanda Seems like it.
Officer Well, they say diamonds are a girl's best friend!

Exercise 1

Read the dialogue and put the sentences in the right order.

a) They opened them. ____
b) A big wave hit the boat. ____
c) Rob contacted the Coast Guard. ____
d) They went to the cabin. ____
e) They discovered some packets. ____
f) A storm started. ____
g) They found lots of diamonds. ____
h) Someone hid some packets of diamonds on the boat. 1
i) Yolanda's camera box broke the wooden panels. ____
j) They repaired some damage to the boat. ____

Exercise 2

What *had happened* before Meg and Yolanda discovered the diamonds? Use the correct verbs to complete these sentences.

1 A storm *had started.*
2 They ________ to their cabin.
3 A big wave ________ the ship.
4 Yolanda's camera box ________ wooden panels.
5 They ________ some packets behind the panels.
6 They ________ the packets.

What *had happened* by the time the customs officer came on board? Complete these sentences.

7 They ________ lots of diamonds.
8 They ________ a bad storm.
9 They ________ some damage to the boat.
10 They ________ the Coast Guard.
11 They ________ in New York.

Exercise 3

Here is Suzy's diary for one day last week. Read it carefully and then ask your partner what Suzy had done by different times during the day, eg

A: What had Suzy done by half-past nine?
B: She had opened and distributed the mail. What had she done by ten o'clock?
A: She had opened and distributed the mail and she had phoned new sponsors. What had she done by eleven o'clock? Etc.

0900-0930	Open and distribute the mail
0930-1000	Phone new sponsors
1000-1100	Take dictation from Geoff Walton
1100-1115	Have a coffee break
1115-1200	Type Geoff Walton's letters
1200-1300	File correspondence
1300-1400	Have lunch with Dave
1400-1500	Type two reports
1500-1600	Go to Air Radio
1600-1630	Order office supplies
1630-1700	Prepare an agenda for a committee meeting

Exercise 4

Prepare a diary like Suzy's for yourself for one day last week. Ask your partner to tell you what they had done by 5 o'clock. Then, from memory, write a paragraph about what your partner had done by the end of the day. When you have finished, compare it with your partner's diary.

LESSON 22

All of Us Were Interviewed

In New York, Meg keeps her diary up-to-date.

SEPTEMBER 20

The boat was inspected by the customs this morning—and so were we! The boat was turned upside down in their search for diamonds and more were found in the other cabins. They said there were enough diamonds to pay the national debt!

All of us were interviewed. I was interrogated twice by a very unpleasant officer. It was like a bad movie. We all feel like criminals. The boat is now under surveillance. We were told to act normally, but how can we?

SEPTEMBER 21

We still have plenty of problems with the crew. Things haven't been the same since Rob was reprimanded by Howard. He's too bossy. Problems, problems!

The customs returned today, and Yolanda and I were interviewed separately by the same officer. Then they went away. I hope they don't come back again!

Jack says that the customs men are hiding. He thinks they are hoping to surprise the real diamond merchants. He thinks the diamonds were hidden on the boat for someone to collect. The customs are watching and waiting for the smuggler or his agent to come and then they will arrest him.

Jack phoned Charles' Manhatten number, but he wasn't there. Jack left a message on the answer phone.

SEPTEMBER 22

Charles turned up today. He arrived with plenty of goodies, including a crate of champagne. He was in a very happy mood. And there was enough food and drink to feed an army!

SEPTEMBER 23

Charles has invited us all to a party. The customs men say we can go. The party's at the Melissa Beach Yacht Club. Fortunately, Chuck Nagner will be there, so at last we can get some media coverage.

Exercise 1

Put the following sentences in the correct order according to the story in Meg's diary.

a) They were told to act normally. ____
b) Charles arrived with lots of food and drink. ____
c) The customs officers returned. ____
d) The boat was inspected. ____
e) Meg was interrogated twice. ____
f) Jack left a message for Charles. ____
g) The crew were invited to a party. ____
h) Meg and Yolanda were interviewed by the same officer. ____
i) The customs officers came to the boat. __1__
j) More diamonds were discovered. ____

Exercise 2

In Exercise 1, there are two types of sentence:

Type 1

The Customs officers *returned*.
Jack *left* a message for Charles.
Charles *arrived* with lots of food.

Type 2

The boat *was inspected*.
The crew *were invited* to a party.
More diamonds *were found*.

Type 1 sentences are in the active voice, and the verbs are in the Past Tense.

Type 2 sentences are in the passive voice, and the verb 'be' is in the ________ Tense, followed by the past participle.

Rule: The Past Passive consists of ________ parts:
(i) the ______ Tense of the verb ________,
(ii) the ________ participle of the main verb,
eg ________ found, were ________,
was ________.

Complete the following sentences with the Past Passive.

1 The ship ________ by the customs.
2 All the crew ________.
3 The boat ________ upside down.
4 More diamonds ________.
5 The crew ________ to act normally.
6 The boat ________ under surveillance.
7 A message ________ for Charles.
8 Everyone ________ to the Melissa Beach Yacht Club.

Exercise 3

Howard and Lisa are checking the ship's stores. Using the information in the table, practise their dialogue with a partner. Take turns at being A and B.

What we've got		What we need
flour	25kg	40kg
sugar	12kg	10kg
oil	5 litres	10 litres
biscuits	10 boxes	20 boxes
coffee	10kg	15kg
oranges	4 doz	10 doz
lemons	3 doz	2 doz
salt	2kg	2kg

A: How much flour have we got?
B: Twenty-five kilos. How much do we need?
A: Forty.
B: So, we haven't got enough flour.
A: No, I'll order some more. What about fruit? How many lemons have we got?
B: Three dozen. How many do we need?
A: Two dozen, so we've got enough. Etc.

Exercise 4

Write a short autobiography, using Past Active and Past Passive verbs. You can use the sentences below where appropriate.

I was born in (place) in (year). I was educated at (name of elementary school) and (name of high school). I left school in (year) and began work at (name of organization). In (year) I met my wife/husband and we were married in (year). We have (number) children. Our first child, (name), was born in (year) and our second, (name), was born in (year). I now work at (name of organization).

LESSON 23

He Shouldn't Have Said That

After the party, Jack and Charles talk.

Jack Well, you remembered to bring lots of goodies, Charles.
Charles Yes but I forgot to bring Yolanda's favourite sandwiches!
Jack Too bad. She enjoyed the smoked salmon – not to mention the champagne.
Charles I'm glad she did. I'll remember to bring salt beef and caviar next time.
Jack And don't forget to bring some more of the amber nectar.
Charles The amber what?
Jack You know – Australian lager.
Charles Oh sure. Anyway, Jack, you've had a pretty eventful journey. And some arguments, too, I hear.
Jack You mean Rob and Howard?
Charles Yes. What happened?
Jack Well, Howard told Rob to do something.
Charles Yes, and then what?
Jack Rob told Howard to get lost.
Charles Oh, he shouldn't have said that.
Jack No, but Howard isn't the captain. Meg is.
Charles Right. And he shouldn't really have given Rob orders.
Jack Then he told Rob to stop wasting time and to do some real work for a change.
Charles He certainly shouldn't have said that.
Jack No, he shouldn't have. Rob's a good bloke. Yolanda was there, and she told Howard to leave Rob alone.
Charles I bet he didn't like that. What did he tell her to do?
Jack He told her to mind her own business.
Charles Well, maybe she shouldn't have interfered. It wasn't really her business. You know, Jack, perhaps I should have come with you, after all.

Exercise 1

Answer the following questions.

1 What did Charles remember to bring?
2 What did he forget to bring?
3 What is 'amber nectar'?
4 Who shouldn't have given Rob orders?
5 Who shouldn't have interfered?
6 Who should have gone with the expedition?

Exercise 2

Complete the following sentences.

1 I remembered ________ some food.
2 I forgot ________ some drink.
3 Don't ________ to bring some champagne!
4 Don't forget ________ some smoked salmon!

Practise this dialogue with a partner. Take turns to be A and B.

A: Don't forget to bring some (1) drink for the party.
B: No, I won't. But don't forget to bring (2) some wine.
A: I won't. After all, last time I remembered to bring (2) some beer.
B: Yes, but then you forgot to get (3) some lemonade.
A: OK, I'll remember this time.

(1) nibbles for the party; flowers for our hostess; food for the picnic*

(2) some beer; some nuts and olives; some roses; some cold chicken*

(3) some ice; some chocolates; some bread*

* Add items of your own.

Exercise 3

Complete the following table.

What X said or did	What X shouldn't have said or done
	He shouldn't have given Rob orders.
Rob told Howard to get lost.	
Yolanda told Howard to leave Rob alone.	
	He shouldn't have said that.

Now comment on the following.

Example:

A: Charles has drunk all the champagne. (thirsty)
B: He shouldn't have drunk it all.
A: Maybe he was thirsty.
B: Perhaps, but he should've asked first.

1 Howard has finished the coffee. (thirsty)
2 Yolanda has taken the car. (in a hurry)
3 Dave has borrowed your tapes. (needed them)
4 Jack has eaten all the bread. (hungry)
5 Suzy has left the windows open. (hot)
6 Rob has drunk all the milk. (thirsty)
7 Jack has used all the eggs. (hungry)
8 Meg has gone for a walk. (needed a break)

Exercise 4

Are there any things you shouldn't have done this week? Make a list of four or five things and give reasons for doing them. Compare your list with a partner and comment on each other's lists.

Examples:

On Monday I shouldn't have lost my temper. But I was very tired.
On Tuesday I shouldn't have eaten some chocolate. But I was very hungry.
On Wednesday I shouldn't have slept in late. But I was very tired. Etc.

LESSON 24

I Wonder If He Will

Exercise 1

Choose True or False. Then write the sentences from the text that give the answers.

1 There were two storms during the voyage.
2 Lisa is surprised when Charles asks about the bathroom.
3 Charles finds six packets in Yolanda's cabin.
4 The police driver is sure that Charles will not see them.
5 The police take Charles' money.
6 The police want Meg to tell the press about the diamonds.

Exercise 2

'Yes/No' questions (questions with 'Yes' or 'No' as the answer).
Read the examples and rules, and complete (i) by giving the missing word.

'*Will they see us?*' 'I wonder if they'll see us?'
'*Does she like me?*' 'I wonder if she likes me?'
'Will they see us?' and 'Does she like me?' are direct 'Yes/No' questions.

Rule: When we change a direct 'Yes/No' question into an indirect question after 'wonder', these changes are made:
(i) We introduce the indirect question with the word ________.
(ii) The verb changes from the question form to the statement form.

Change the following into indirect questions beginning with 'I wonder if. . . . .'

1 Does Robert think about his old girlfriend?
2 Does Meg feel happy?
3 Are the team enjoying themselves in New York?
4 Will the police catch all the smugglers?
5 Is Charles one of the smugglers?

'Wh-' questions (why, when, where, who, how, etc.).
Read the examples and complete the rule.

'*Why is he asking again?*' 'I wonder why he's asking again.'
'*When did he come?*' 'I wonder when he came.'

Rule: 'Why is he asking again?' and 'When did he come?' are direct 'wh-' questions. We change a direct 'wh-' question into an indirect question after 'wonder' as follows:
(i) The question word remains the same.
(ii) The verb changes from the question form to the ________ form.

Change the following into indirect questions beginning with 'I wonder . . .'

1 Why did Charles visit the boat?
2 Who is Cornelius?
3 Where did the diamonds come from?
4 Where will the police take Charles?
5 How are the police going to catch all the smugglers?

Exercise 3

Make lists of the nouns that follow 'a good deal of', 'a lot of', and 'a good many of'. Complete the rule.
We had a good deal of fine weather./There was a lot of damage./We met a good many of his contacts./I read a lot of the book./I read a good many of the books./I like a lot of old films./ I missed a lot of the film.

Rule:
(i) 'a good deal of' is followed by a singular noun.
(ii) 'a good many of' is followed by plural nouns.
(iii) 'a lot of' is followed by either ________ nouns, or ________ nouns.

Put 'a good deal of' or 'a good many of' in front of the following:

1 the anger, **2** the policemen, **3** the ocean, **4** the surprise, **5** the dogs, **6** the doubt

Exercise 4

Think about future possibilities for you or others. Write five sentences beginning

'*I wonder if I'll . . . . .*' or
'*I wonder if . . . . . will . . . . .*'

LESSON 25

I Wish I Was Wrong

Otto Bergman is worried because Charles Durberville hasn't contacted him. He phones Bernie Castello, who works for him in New York, to find out if there is any news.

Bergman Where is Charles Durberville, Bernie?
Castello I'm not sure.
Bergman What do you mean?
Castello Well, I'm certain that I saw him on the *Ocean Explorer* when it left New York.
Bergman That's impossible!
Castello I saw him . . . . . or a man who looked like him, and he was on the deck of the yacht when it pulled out.
Bergman I wish I was in New York right now. If I was there, I'd soon find out the truth. Look, tell me the story again. You say that you saw Charles and Cornelius before they went to collect the diamonds from the yacht.
Castello That's right. It was all planned. Cornelius was going to do the talking while Charles collected the diamonds.
Bergman So they got the diamonds and drove to the motel. Did you see them after they collected the money at the motel?
Castello No, I didn't.
Bergman So there's no money and there are no diamonds.
Castello I wish I was wrong, Mr Bergman, but I'm telling you . . . . . Charlie was on the yacht.
Bergman That crook! He's stolen the diamonds and he's going to sell them privately. I'll teach him to double-cross me.
Castello If it's true, it means that Meg Brooke and her crew are helping him. They're all involved.
Bergman Yes, but they're wrong if they think they can cheat me. Sam's in the Caribbean, isn't he? I'll get him to prepare a little surprise for them when they arrive. We'll make sure they never see their Institute again.

Exercise 1

Read the dialogue and choose the correct ending for the sentences below.

1 Otto Bergman is talking . . . . . F
2 Bernie is certain that he saw Charles . . . . . ____
3 A man who looked like Charles . . . . . ____
4 Bernie saw Charles and Cornelius before . . . . . ____
5 Cornelius and Charles got . . . . . ____
6 Bernie didn't see Charles and Cornelius after . . . . . ____
7 Otto believes that Charles . . . . . ____
8 Otto is sure that Meg and her crew . . . . . ____
9 Otto will get Sam to prepare a surprise for the crew . . . . . ____

a) . . . . . when they arrive in the Caribbean.
b) . . . . . has stolen the diamonds.
c) . . . . . they collected the money at the motel.
d) . . . . . was on the deck of the yacht when it pulled out.
e) . . . . . are helping Charles.
f) . . . . . to Bernie Castello.
g) . . . . . on the *Ocean Explorer* when it left New York.
h) . . . . . they went to collect the diamonds from the yacht.
i) . . . . . the diamonds and drove to the motel.

Rule: Study this example:
'I haven't got the diamonds. *I wish I had them.*'
If you regret that something is not true, you use 'I ________' + noun or pronoun + Past Simple.

Study this example:

'There isn't any news from Charles.
I wish he would phone.'
If we want someone to do something we can use 'I wish' + noun or pronoun + ________ + verb.

Exercise 2

Complete the sentences. Use the words in brackets.

Examples:

Otto is in Britain, but he *wishes he was in New York.* (New York)
I haven't had any news from my girlfriend. I *wish she would write.* (write)

1 Otto is right, but he ____________. (be wrong)
2 Bernie Castello doesn't like working in New York. He __________. (work in the Caribbean)
3 Charles is on the *Ocean Explorer*. Otto wishes Charles ________ on the *Ocean Explorer*. (not be)
4 Rob uses Howard's toothpaste. Howard _____. (not use it)
5 Otto hasn't got the money for the diamonds. He ______________. (get the money for them)
6 Howard and Rob are arguing. Meg ______. (not argue)
7 Rob only buys egg sandwiches. Yolanda _____. (buy salt beef sandwiches)
8 Otto has a problem and he doesn't know the answer. He ______________. (know the answer)

Exercise 3

Complete the dialogue with the phrases below.

take the number of the getaway car
call the police
saw a robbery
a pencil and paper
the police didn't come
chase the thieves

A: What would you do if you _________?
B: I'd _________. What would you do?
A: I'd _________.
B: What would you do if _________?
A: I'd _________.
B: I'd do the same if I had _________.

Practise the dialogue with your partner, then use these phrases to make another dialogue.

take a holiday; lost your job; start my own business; there was no work; enough money; look for another job

Invent other dialogues like this one.

Exercise 4

Complete these sentences. Compare your ideas with your partner's.

If I were a politician, I . . . . .
If I spoke English very well . . . . .
If I owned an aeroplane . . . . .
If I had enough money . . . . .
If I discovered a valuable painting . . . . .

LESSON 26

I Could Repair a Boat When I Was Twelve

CRITICS EXPRESS DOUBTS ABOUT *OCEAN EXPLORER* CREW

Can the *Ocean Explorer* crew succeed? Can a group of amateurs really manage to get round the world? Have they got the stamina and the knowledge? These are some of the questions that sailing enthusiasts are asking as the *Ocean Explorer* – the International Ocean Institute's research vessel – sets out on the next stage of its journey.

But are these amateurs really as inexperienced as their critics say? 'Anyone who says that we're inexperienced is talking nonsense', says Jack Craig, the 53-year-old *Ocean Explorer* navigator and round-the-world sailor. 'I could sail a dinghy single-handed when I was ten years old . . . and I still can. I could repair a boat when I was twelve and build one when I was fourteen. Am I really inexperienced?'

Craig's five colleagues have suffered severe criticism. After only a few weeks at sea there are rumours of disagreements between *Ocean Explorer* captain, Meg Brooke, and her second-in-command, Howard Ellway. A power struggle? A war of the sexes? Craig wants to stop these rumours. 'We managed to complete the first stage of the journey, didn't we? And we managed it without major problems!'

But many questions are still unanswered. The crew now face a voyage of several months. How does a team of three men and three women work together harmoniously? Is it true that top photographer, Yolanda Richmond, is now focusing on radio operator Robert Adair? 'This is an expedition, not a party', says Craig. 'If I were you, I'd get my facts right.'

Exercise 1

Make these statements correct. Copy the sentences from the magazine story that give the correct answer.

1 The reporter believes that the *Ocean Explorer* crew members are professional sailors.

____

2 Jack says that the crew are inexperienced.

____

3 Jack knew how to sail a dinghy when he was five.

____

4 Jack knew how to fix a boat when he was fourteen.

____

5 The crew didn't finish the first part of the journey.

____

6 The rest of the journey will take a few weeks.

____

Exercise 2

Rule: I *could ride* a bicycle when I was six.
To describe some ability you had in the past, you use '________' + verb.

Now complete the following sentences about yourself.

1 I ______________ when I was two years old.
2 When I was seven, I ______________.
3 I ______________ when I was ten.

Exercise 3

Many things were difficult for the *Ocean Explorer* team. What did they *manage to do* successfully? Write full sentences and make any necessary changes. Use these notes.

> *The team – completed the first stage of the journey*
> *The team managed to complete the first leg of the journey.*

1 Meg – found some sponsors

____

2 Rob – joined the crew

____

3 Yolanda – took some interesting photographs

____

4 Howard – stayed calm

____

5 Lisa – improved her cooking

____

Exercise 4

Practise this dialogue with your partner.

A: We can't go/eat. The car/cooker isn't working.
B: It's all right. I managed to start/repair it.
A: We haven't got any petrol/bread.
B: Yes, we have. I managed to get some this morning.
A: Are you sure you can drive/cook?
B: Of course! I could drive/cook when I was thirteen/ten years old.

Now make up similar dialogues. Here are some topics:

watching football on TV
going to a party
washing your hair

Exercise 5

Make a list of questions like this:

When could you read/swim/drive a car?
What things could you do when you were three/eight/fifteen?

When you have finished, use your questions to interview different members of your class. Make a note of their answers. Then write a short report from your notes.

Write sentences like this:

Caterina could read when she was five, but Juan could read when he was four.

LESSON 27

The Girl Who's Looking at the Camera Equipment

Yolanda is shopping in Miami.

Assistant 1 I think it's her.
Assistant 2 Who?
Assistant 1 The girl who's standing over there.
Assistant 2 Which girl? There are two.
Assistant 1 The girl who's looking at the camera equipment.
Assistant 2 Oh, that one. Are you sure?
Assistant 1 Quiet! She's coming this way.

*****

Assistant 1 Can I help you?
Yolanda Yes, please. I want some film for my camera. I can't find the film I usually buy.
Assistant 1 Is it for slides, colour, black and white. . . . . ?
Yolanda All three. This is the film I bought last time.
Assistant 1 Let's see. Oh, yes, we've got plenty of this in stock. How many rolls do you need?
Yolanda A hundred of each, please.
Assistant 1 A hundred! Are you doing some kind of modelling assignment? You look like a model.
Yolanda No, I'm not.
Assistant 1 Haven't I seen you somewhere before?
Yolanda No, I don't think so.
Assistant 1 You're the one who does that quiz programme on television. What's it called? Oh, yes . . . . . 'Easy Money'.
Yolanda No, I'm not.
Assistant 1 Well, I'm sure I've seen you somewhere before.
Yolanda I'm sure you haven't.
Assistant 1 I know! You're the actress who plays opposite Chris Cerino in 'The Incredible Man'.
Yolanda No, really, I'm not.
Assistant 1 You're a singer.
Yolanda No.
Assistant 1 You're the singer who threw that chat show host into a swimming pool last year. Now I remember. You know, that's the best thing I've seen on TV for years.
Yolanda No, you're wrong. Look, I'm just an ordinary girl who's going to take some ordinary photos on an ordinary holiday. And now, if you don't mind, I'll buy my film somewhere else. Goodbye.

Exercise 1

The assistant in the department store thinks he has recognized Yolanda. How is she described? Read the dialogue and complete the sentences.

1 The girl who's standing over there.
2 __________ threw that chat show host into a swimming pool last year.
3 The girl __________.
4 __________ plays opposite Chris Cerino in 'The Incredible Man'.
5 You're the one __________.
6 ______ going to take some ordinary photos on an ordinary holiday.

Exercise 2

Join these sentences with 'who' or 'that'.

Example:

This is the yacht. It sailed to the USA from Britain.

This is the yacht that sailed to the USA from Britain.

Otto Bergman is a boatyard owner. He lent the yacht to the Institute.

Otto Bergman is a boatyard owner who lent the yacht to the Institute.

1 These are the sandwiches. They taste so delicious.

____

2 Jack is the navigator. He could repair a boat when he was twelve.

____

3 Meg is the marine biologist. She went to Florida last May.

____

4 This is the fax. It arrived last night from Dr Walton.

____

5 Lisa is the Dutch girl. She is a research student at the Institute.

____

6 There's the dog. It bites people.

____

Rule: Study these examples:

She's the woman *who won the Marathon.*
This is the computer *that can do everything.*

We can describe someone or ________ with a relative clause. A relative clause usually begins with 'who' when it refers to a person. It begins with ________ when it refers to a thing or animal.

Exercise 3

Practise this dialogue with your partner.

A: Are you the person who owns the red sports car/Alsatian dog?
B: No, I'm not. Are you the lady/gentleman who had the accident/got bitten?
A: No, my friend's the one who is in hospital/made the complaint.
B: So you're the person who called the ambulance/telephoned the police, are you?
A: Yes, that's right. Who are you?
B: I'm the woman/man who saw the car crash/attack.

Invent some other dialogues like this one. Here are some ideas to start you off. Talk about:

the student who passed the French exam
the actor who was on television last night
the man/woman who sailed around the world

Exercise 4

Think of five people who are well-known in your country. Write their names on a piece of paper and give it to your partner. He/she must say who the people are. For example:

Tom Cruise. He's the American actor who starred in 'Rain Man'.

Now, on a separate piece of paper, write similar sentences about yourself. Don't write your name. Write sentences like this:

I'm the student who has a job in an office.
I'm the student who has an older brother.

Mix up all the descriptions. Can you guess who wrote each description?

LESSON 28

It's Moving Very Quickly

Exercise 1

Put the following sentences in the correct order according to the text.

a) Howard jumped into the water with Meg. ____
b) Someone removed the warning sign at the Green Lagoon. __1__
c) Rob saved Lisa and Yolanda with the inflatable. ____
d) Jack and Rob saw a shark. ____
e) The *Ocean Explorer* arrived at the Green Lagoon. ____
f) They told a man about their adventure. ____
g) Jack went to help Meg and Howard. ____
h) Lisa and Yolanda dived into the lagoon. ____

Exercise 2

'He *sometimes* behaves childishly.' 'He *often* writes letters.'

Rule: When the verb is in the Present Simple:
(i) adverbs which say *how often* something happens usually (but not always) come ________ the verb.
Notice the position with the negative:
'He doesn't *always* behave badly.'

'He sometimes behaves *childishly*.'
'It's moving towards them very *quickly*.'
(ii) adverbs which say *how* something happens usually come ________ the verb, and the object.

Rewrite the following, with the adverbs in the usual position.

1 Meg worries about the journey. (often)
2 Jack drinks. (sometimes) (heavily)
3 Robert doesn't get up early. (always)
4 Lisa prepares their breakfast. (usually) (quickly)
5 Yolanda takes photographs. (carefully) (always)
6 The team doesn't sing songs. (loudly) (often)
7 Howard doesn't obey Jack's orders. (very quickly) (often)
8 Robert listens to the weather forecast. (carefully) (always)

Exercise 3

Read the dialogue and then construct similar dialogues with a partner. Some phrases are given to help you. Take turns to be A and B.

A: I can't (1) ski at all. But my friends always (1) ski (2) perfectly.
B: We can't do everything. But you (1) swim very well, don't you?
A: I suppose so. What about you? Don't you (1) swim very well?
B: Oh no, I (3) usually (1) swim very (4) slowly.

(1) swim; play football; play basketball; sew; knit; play chess; play cards; sail; windsurf

(2) brilliantly; superbly; wonderfully

(3) always; normally; frequently; often

(4) badly; poorly; carelessly

Exercise 4

Write about some things that you do. Say how often you do them (sometimes, frequently, etc.), and in what way you do them (perfectly, badly, slowly, etc.).

LESSON 29

I'll Take Both of Them

Howard and Meg go to a local restaurant for a drink and a meal.

Waiter What would you like, sir?
Howard Meg?
Meg I'd like a scotch, please.
Howard Yes, so would I. Whiskies for both of us, please. With lots of ice.

The waiter leaves.

Meg I'm very hungry. I'd like to order something to eat.
Howard Yes, I'd like to have something, too. Let's relax and forget our problems for a while.
Meg Oh, Howard, look at that souvenir seller over there.
Seller Can I be of service, madam? I have the best and the cheapest souvenirs. Would you like to see my magic necklaces? They're very special. And very beautiful.
Meg I'd like to look at those ones, please.
Seller Certainly, madam. Here you are.
Meg They're very pretty. What do you think, Howard?
Howard They're lovely. And the shells are very delicate.
Seller If you take both of the pink ones, I can give you a special price. You are very special people.
Howard And you are very persuasive. I'll take both of them.
Meg But I'm buying them, Howard.
Howard Oh, no you're not. I am. For you. As a souvenir of our escape from danger.
Meg Howard, thank you. That's really nice of you.
Waiter Here are your drinks. With lots of ice.
Howard Thanks. And now, Meg, here's to both of us.
Seller Don't forget me, sir. I think my necklaces have a special magic for a special price.

Exercise 1

Answer the following questions.

1 How many whiskies did Howard order?
2 How could Howard obtain a special price?
3 What did the souvenir seller think about Howard and Meg?
4 How many necklaces did Howard buy?
5 Did Meg accept Howard's gift?
6 What had Howard forgotten to do?

Exercise 2

Complete this table.

Number	Pattern
________	none of them/us
1	________
________	both of them/us
________	all/several of them/us

Practise the dialogue with a partner. Take turns to be A and B.

A: Look at these (1) medallions.
B: Oh, yes. Which ones do you like?
A: (2) The gold ones.
B: I prefer the (2) silver ones. Let's buy (3) one of them.
A: OK. I'll take (4) the small gold one.
B: Yes, and I'll take (4) the big silver one.

(1) bracelets; earrings; necklaces; baskets; bags*

(2) the silver ones; the big ones; the little ones*

(3) both of them; several of them; all of them

(4) the big silver one; the small gold one; the large decorated one; the small leather one*

* Add information of your own.

Exercise 3

Less Polite	More Polite
What do you want? I want X.	What would you like? I would like X. (I'd like)

Rule: When we want to be polite, we use
'________' plus verb., eg
'________ *you like X? I* ________ *like X.*'
To make a polite offer, we say:
What ________?
To make a polite request, we say:
I ________ *like X, please.*

Find examples of these patterns in the dialogue. Make these sentences polite.

1 I want a gin and tonic.
2 Do you want ice with your drink?
3 What do you want to eat?
4 I want a steak and salad.
5 What salad dressing do you want?
6 I want blue cheese dressing.

Exercise 4

Read this puzzle and answer the questions. Then write a similar puzzle of your own and exchange it with your partner.

Lisa and Jack went souvenir shopping. Lisa liked the seashell necklaces, so she bought three of them. They cost three dollars each. Jack bought none of them. Then they saw some T shirts. Jack bought two of them. Lisa bought one. They cost five dollars each. How much did Lisa spend? How much did Jack spend?

LESSON 30

If We Changed Our Route, We Might Avoid Difficulties

Meg is worried about the safety of the boat and crew. She sends a fax to Geoffrey, proposing route changes.

From: Meg Brooke

To: Geoffrey Walton, Director

Re: Route changes

Because of the problems we have had, I think it would be a good idea to change our route. Someone is trying to get us. First, there were the diamonds and then there was the shark. If we changed our route, we might avoid further difficulties. We are thinking about sailing across the South Atlantic to Australia via South Africa. If we did that, we would avoid Latin America where we might have major problems.

Regards from us all. Meg

From: Geoffrey Walton, Director
To: Meg Brooke
Re: Alterations to route

Route changes might cause problems. If you made big changes, we could have difficulties with our sponsors. For example, if you avoided Recife, you wouldn't see Carlos Coutou. A visit to the Oceanographic Institute there is very important. Likewise, if you by-passed Rio, you would lose important contacts and publicity.

I suggest that you keep to the original route. After all, if you sailed across the South Atlantic, you would be weeks at sea. I suggest that you file false sailing plans. If there was a gang after you, the false plans might fool them. So you could announce new plans and then keep to the original itinerary. That might put them off the scent.

Best wishes

Geoffrey

From: Meg Brooke

To: Geoffrey Walton

Re: Sailing plans

Thanks for your advice. We have given false plans at the port. We have said that we are sailing direct to Punta del Este in Uruguay. In fact, we will call at Recife and Rio in Brazil on the way south. Please publish our false plans, because they might deceive our pursuers. Meanwhile, we hope to arrive safely in Brazil.

All the best, Meg

Exercise 1

Read the texts and complete the sentences.

1 Meg wants to change the route in order to ________.
2 Geoff doesn't want her to change the route in order to ________.
3 If they missed Recife, they ________ Carlos Coutou.
4 If they bypassed Rio, they ________.
5 If they sailed across the South Atlantic, ________.

(1) live dangerously; visit somewhere different; learn a new language; have a new experience

(2) travelled in the Amazon jungle, you could live dangerously; visited the Yemen, you could go somewhere different; studied Chinese, you could learn a new language; took up hang-gliding, you could have a new experience

(3) like it? be successful? be safe?

(4) try it; give it a go

Exercise 2

Study these sentences.

'If' clause: condition	**Main clause: result**
If we changed our route,	we might avoid further difficulties.
If you sailed across the South Atlantic,	you would be weeks at sea.

Complete the following rule.

Rule: In these examples, we use the ________ Tense in the 'If' clause, and modal verbs like '________' or '________' plus verb in the main clause.

This type of sentence can be used to express how certain the speaker is.

Quite certain	**Uncertain**
would	might

Match the two parts of these sentences.

1 If your brother worked harder, ...
2 If he passed the exam, ...
3 If your sister took another course, ...
4 If you changed jobs, ...

a) . . . . . he would pass his exam.
b) . . . . . she might be happier.
c) . . . . . he might be promoted.
d) . . . . . you might save more money.

Exercise 3

Practise the dialogue with a partner. Take turns at being A and B.

A: I want to (1) visit some ancient ruins.
B: If you (2) went to Egypt, you could visit lots of ancient ruins.
A: But would I (3) enjoy it?
B: You might not (3) enjoy it, but I'm sure you would (1) see some ancient ruins.
A: OK. Well, maybe I'll (4) go there.

Exercise 4

Here are some changes in people's habits or ways of life.

changing jobs
going somewhere different for a vacation
giving up a habit like smoking or drinking
taking up a new hobby or sport
joining a club, eg a tennis or golf club
buying a new car

Choose one of these and make a list of the advantages and disadvantages which the changes might bring, eg more interesting activities or people, reduced or added expenditure, greater or less convenience, improvement to health, etc. Then find someone who wants to make the change you have chosen, and give them advice. Example:

A: I'd like to change my job.
B: Why?
A: I want to do something more interesting.
B: If you changed your job, you might do something more interesting and you would meet new people. Is that the only reason you want to change jobs?
A: No, it isn't. I'd like to earn more money, too.
B: Well, you might earn more money, but you might have more expenses, too.
A: Yes, that's right. Thanks for your advice.

LESSON 31

That's the One I Mean

Simon (at a telephone) OK, Mr Bergman, I'll keep an eye on them.

*****

In London, Dave and Suzy go out for a drink, and they meet someone with a secret.

Suzy Dave, look at the chap over there!
Dave Which chap? The one with the funny hat? Is that the one you mean?
Suzy No, I mean the guy in the black leather jacket.
Dave The one who's standing next to the door?
Suzy Yes, that's the one I mean. He keeps looking at us.
Dave I'm not surprised. The person you're looking at is a friend. Come and meet him.
Simon Hi, Dave. Who's the bird?
Suzy I'm not a bird.
Simon Oops, sorree!
Dave Simon, this is Suzy. Suzy – Simon.
Suzy Hi, Simon. Haven't we met before?
Simon I don't think so, darling. Can I get you a drink?
Suzy I'm driving, so I'll have a mineral water, please.
Simon Dave?
Dave A pint of bitter.
Simon Mineral water, a pint of bitter and a blackjack please, love.
Simon Well, here's to us all.
Dave, Suzy Cheers.
Dave What's that you're drinking, Simon?
Simon A blackjack.
Suzy It looks disgusting. What is it?
Simon That's a secret.
Suzy I'm sure you've got lots of secrets, Simon.

Exercise 1

Answer the following:

1 Who is Simon going to 'keep an eye on'?
2 The person Suzy means is wearing __________.
3 Suzy thinks that she has __________ before.
4 Suzy
  a) doesn't like being called 'a bird'.
  b) likes being called 'a bird'.
  c) doesn't mind being called 'a bird'.
5 Why does Suzy ask for a mineral water?
6 Suzy thinks that Simon has __________.

Exercise 2

There are three patterns in the dialogue. Complete the examples with words from the dialogue.

Pattern

1 The + noun + 'with' + noun
Example: ____________________
2 The + noun + 'in' + noun
Example: ____________________
3 The + 'one' + 'who/which' + verb
Example: ____________________

To identify someone or something, we use the above patterns.

Match the two parts of the sentences below.

I mean the car	in a mink coat.
the woman	with a Swiss numberplate.
the house	with a fur collar.
the man	with a red front door.
the girl	with a grey beard.
the coat	with long blonde hair.

Exercise 3

Practise this dialogue. Take turns to be A and B.

A: Do you know (1) Mike?
B: I'm not sure. Who do you mean? The (2) chap with short red hair?
A: No, not really. I mean the one (3) with long black hair.
B: Oh, that isn't (1) Mike. It's (4) Tom.
A: Well, (5) he's very attractive.

(1) Lisa, Charles, Yolanda, Geoff*

(2) the girl in a black dress; the chap in a brown sweater; the girl in a red dress; the man in a light suit*

(3) the one in a green skirt; the one in a grey jacket; the girl in a black dress; the chap in a dark suit*

(4) Meg, Jack, Suzy, Howard*

(5) she's very pretty; he's very handsome; she's very amusing; he's very important*

* Use your own information.

Exercise 4

Write a short description of someone in your class on a slip of paper. Put the slips together, and then read the slips one by one. Try to guess the name of the person described.

Example:

The person I mean is the one in a red sweater. She comes from Milan and she is very attractive.

The person I mean is the one with short, dark hair. He is a salesman and he is very important.

LESSON 32

It's a Pity We're Late

Exercise 1

Answer the following questions.

1 Why does Lisa say 'It's lucky that we're near a petrol station'?
2 Can Howard speak Portuguese?
3 Can Yolanda speak Portuguese?
4 Which two people were arguing?
5 Why does Howard say 'That's no light, Lisa'?
6 Was there a lot of damage in Lisa's cabin?
7 Who has decided to pay for the damage?
8 What does Howard wonder?

Exercise 2

'*It's lucky (that)* we're near a garage.'
'*It's a pity (that)* you didn't pay them more money.'

Read the example below, then rewrite sentences 1 to 8 in the same way, using 'It's lucky (that) . . . . .' or 'It's a pity (that) . . . . .' depending on the meaning.

Example:

Their car won't start, but they're near a garage.
It's lucky that they're near a garage.

1 It rained all the time when we were at the Boat Race.
2 Robert dropped his wallet, but an honest man found it and returned it.
3 Meg wanted to talk to Geoffrey, but he was not at home when she telephoned.
4 There wasn't any wind when we went windsurfing last weekend.
5 Howard saw the fire before there was much damage.
6 I enjoyed the film, but unfortunately I missed the last bus home.
7 We went skiing but there wasn't enough snow.
8 I lost the key to my house, but the window was open, so I climbed in.

Exercise 3

Study the dialogue. In pairs use the words given to make similar dialogues. Take turns to be A and B.

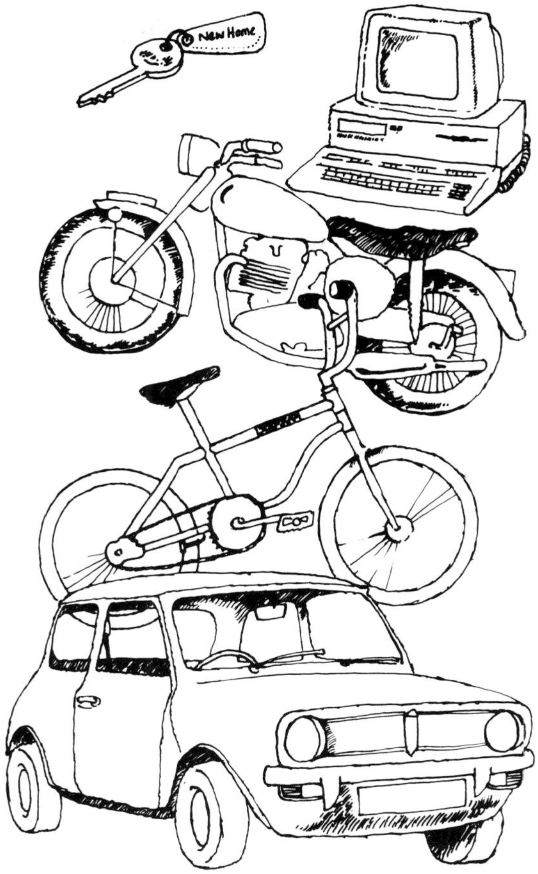

A: What's your new (1) car like?
B: It seems (2) faster than the last one.
A: (3) Good, I'm glad to hear it.

(1) book; motorbike; computer; bicycle; house

(2) more interesting; noisier; better; slower; bigger

(3) Oh dear, I'm sorry to hear it;

'Good, I'm glad to hear it.

(Now make dialogues with your own words.)

Exercise 4

Imagine that you move to a different town (village, etc.). Write a letter to your family, telling them about your first impressions of the town, and compare things to the old town.

You may write about the town, the shops, your flat/house, your neighbours, etc. You can use

'. . . . . *seems* . . . . . *than* . . . . .'

LESSON 33

We'll Wait until after Lunch

Meg and Carlos Couto are on board the *Ocean Explorer*.

Meg Well, thanks for coming to give us a hand, Carlos. We really appreciate it.
Carlos It's a pleasure, Meg. It's the least I can do. I just hope there won't be any more problems.
Meg I hope so, too, Carlos. Is there any news from the police?
Carlos No, nothing, I'm afraid. They have a few ideas, but it's impossible to find witnesses. They'll continue the investigations until they get some answers. How about you? When will you leave?
Meg Quite soon, I hope, but there are a few repairs to do first.
Carlos How long will the work take?
Meg Just a day or two. Right now Jack and Rob are buying supplies and spare parts in town. Howard's mending a few things in Lisa's cabin and Lisa and Yolanda are doing some painting.
Carlos You seem very organized.
Meg We are. Come on, I'll show you.

*****

Meg Yolanda! Lisa! Howard! What are you doing?
Yolanda Nothing.
Meg I can see that. But why?
Lisa It's too hot to work, Meg.
Howard Anyway, we're tired. We worked all day yesterday and the day before.
Yolanda Yes, and we can't do anything until Jack and Rob come back with the tools and equipment.
Lisa We'll wait until after lunch.
Howard Then I'll repair the damage in Lisa's cabin.
Yolanda And until Howard finishes that job, I'll sit here in the shade with Lisa.
Carlos I hate to say this, Meg. At this rate you won't leave Brazil until Christmas.

Exercise 1

Read the dialogue and complete these sentences.

1 Carlos hopes there ____________________.
2 The police will continue the investigations ____________________.
3 Meg and her crew ____________ quite soon.
4 The work ____________ just a day or two.
5 Yolanda, Howard and Lisa can't do anything ____________________.
6 Lisa and the others will wait ____________.
7 Yolanda will sit in the shade with Lisa ____________________ the job.
8 Meg ____________ Brazil ____________.

Rule: Study this example.

Antonio will study until he passes that exam.

Now answer these questions.

Has Antonio passed the exam?
Yes/No
Will he study before he passes the exam?
Yes/No
Will he study after he passes the exam?
Yes/No

The clause that follows 'until' marks a point in time. We use the ________ Tense in the clause that begins with 'until'.

Exercise 2

We've given you the answers. Write the questions. Use the dialogue to help you.

What *will the police do?*
They'll continue their investigations.

1 When ____________________?
Quite soon.
2 What ____________________?
The tools and equipment.
3 When ____________________?
After lunch.
4 Where ____________________?
In the shade.
5 Who ____________________?
Meg won't.

Exercise 3

Practise this dialogue with a partner. Take turns to be A and B.

A: Thanks for coming to give me a hand.
B: It's a pleasure. When will you (1) sell your old car?
A: Quite soon, I hope, but there (2) are some repairs to do first.
B: How long will (3) the repairs take?
A: Just a day or two, but I can't do the (3) repairs until I buy (4) the spare parts.
B: You seem very organized.

(1) move into your new flat; write your report; do your ironing?

(2) is some painting; is some research; is some washing

(3) painting; research; washing

(4) the paint; a new typewriter; some more washing powder

Exercise 4

Write a letter to a friend in England about what you will do next Friday.

Dear ____________
You asked me about my plans for Friday. Well, in the morning I'll ____________________, but I won't ____________________ until ____________________.

I can't ____________________ until ____________________ because ____________________.

Later I ____________________ and then I ____________________ until ____________________.

If you want to come, phone me.
Best wishes

LESSON 34

Nobody Has Complained

1st October
ATTENTION G.W.

This fax comes to you from Rio. We arrived here late last night and have now prepared this up-date on our progress.

First of all, the yacht is in good shape. Everyone has worked very hard since the fire and now everything is running smoothly again.
Unfortunately, we're all a little nervous. The police have confirmed that the last incident was arson. Someone wants to get us and we don't know who or why. I think there is a link between the diamonds and the sabotage attempts. Everybody on board is tired and irritable because they are worried about the dangers of a surprise attack. Despite this, nobody has complained (not even Howard) and no one has asked to leave the expedition. We're a great crew and nothing will stop us now.

We have to change our time schedule because of the fire. Here are the new details:

10th October	Criciuma
15th October	Montevideo
17th October	Buenos Aires
23rd October	Miramar
27th October	Deseado
29th October	Bahia Grande
1st November	Rio Grande
4th November	Cape Horn

There will be colder weather in the south so we'll stop a few days longer in Buenos Aires or Miramar to buy some warm clothes and blankets. We lost some of our winter things in the fire. Will the insurance company pay for the replacements?

We'll send you another fax, or telephone you, as soon as we reach Buenos Aires.

Best wishes,

JC . MB

JC & MB

Rio de Janeiro

Exercise 1

Choose True or False. Rewrite the sentences that are False.

1 The fax is from Jack and Meg to Geoffrey.

____

2 The *Ocean Explorer* arrived in Rio on 1st October.

____

3 The crew is relaxed and happy.

____

4 The *Ocean Explorer* will be in Montevideo on 15th October.

____

5 The crew will buy some summer clothes in Buenos Aires or Miramar.

____

6 Meg and Jack will send the next fax on 17th October.

____

Exercise 2

Rule: 'Everyone' has the same meaning as ________.
________ has the same meaning as 'Nobody'. 'Everyone/Everybody, No one/Nobody', and 'Everything' and 'Nothing' are followed by a ________ verb, not by a plural verb. In sentences with 'No one, Nobody', and 'Nothing', the verb is never negative. It is always ________.

Read the fax. Answer the questions.

1 Who is tired and irritable? ______
2 Who has asked to leave the expedition? ______
3 What will stop the crew? ______
4 Who has worked very hard? ______
5 What is running smoothly again? ______
6 Who has complained? ______

Exercise 3

Choose the correct word.

Dave What's the matter, Suzy?
Suzy *Nothing/Everything* is running smoothly this week.
Dave Why not?
Suzy Well, Dr Walton can't find a copy of the fax from Rio. *Everything/Everybody* is looking for it, but *no one/everyone* can find it.
Dave But you always file *everything/nothing*, don't you?
Suzy Yes. I'm sure I put the fax in the Memo file, but *no one/everybody* believes me because there's *nothing/nobody* there.
Dave Don't worry, Suzy. *No one/Everyone* knows you are a very efficient person.

When you've checked your answers, practise the dialogue with your partner.

Exercise 4

Here are some symbols from a weather map.

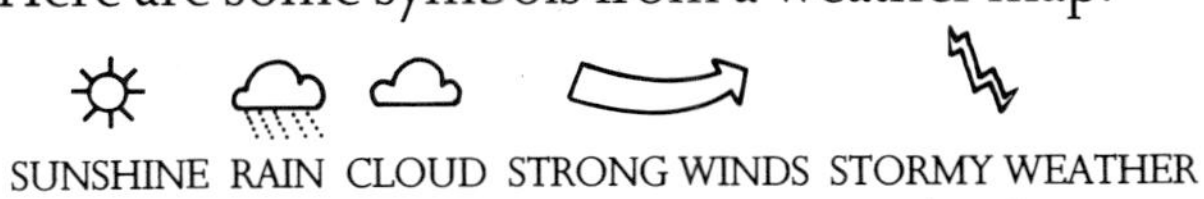

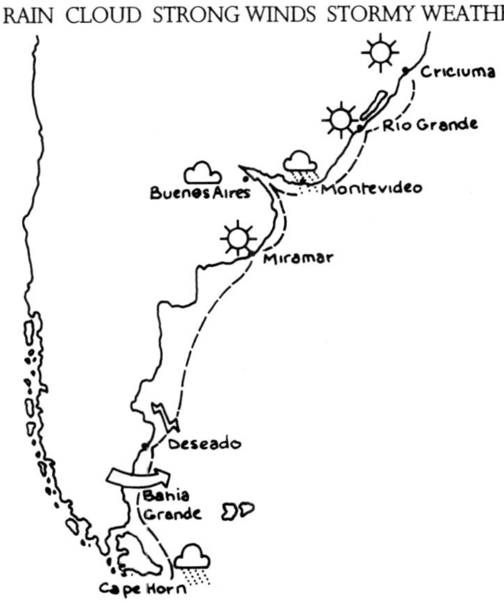

Look at the map of the *Ocean Explorer*'s route. Carlos Couto has given Meg this long-range weather report. Fill in the missing words.

There will be (1) ________ in Criciuma when the *Ocean Explorer* arrives on (2) ________. Then, on 15th October, when you arrive in (3) ________ there will be (4) ________. (5) ________ cloud in Buenos Aires, but there will be (6) ________ in Miramar. On the 27th October, there (7) ________ in (8) ________ and strong winds in (9) ________. On 1st November, the (10) ________ improve and (11) ________ sunshine in (12) ________, but when you reach Cape Horn (13) ________.

Ask your partner to make a list of places to visit. Write him/her a long-range weather forecast. Advise your partner about what clothes to take.

LESSON 35

You'll Have to Hurry

Dorothy Goodness, you're busy today, Suzy.

Suzy Yes, I am. I have to post a million letters and send a fax to Meg. I'll never manage it.

Dorothy Why must you rush? Can't the letters and the fax wait until tomorrow morning?

Suzy I wish they could, but everything's important – especially the fax. It's our list of contacts in the Pacific Islands. Are you good at solving problems, Mrs Walton?

Dorothy I may be. Why?

Suzy Well, I must leave here early in order to meet Dave at six. If I take the fax to the Grosvenor Express office, I'll miss the post office and I'll probably be late for my appointment with Dave, too. So, what's the solution?

Dorothy Easy. Take the letters to the post office and I'll phone Grosvenor Express. I'll ask them to send a messenger to collect the fax.

Suzy I didn't know they had messengers.

Dorothy Suzy! Where have you been for the past twelve months? Geoffrey always calls them when he has to send an urgent message. Now, off you go. You'll have to hurry because the post office closes in ten minutes.

*****

Suzy I'm back.

Dorothy You were quick.

Suzy That's because I ran all the way. How did you get on?

Dorothy Fine. The despatch rider will be here any minute. In fact, I think this is him now. Hello, how are you today?

Simon Very well, thank you, Mrs Walton.

Suzy But you're . . .

Simon Yes, I'm Simon. Hi, Suzy, how are you?

Suzy I . . . I didn't know . . . I mean . . . Do you work for . . ?

Simon For the Grosvenor Express office? Yes, I do.

Dorothy Are you going to give Simon the fax, Suzy?

Suzy No. I mean, . . yes.

Simon Don't worry. I'll take care of it. It will be in good hands.

Exercise 1

Fill the spaces. Use the appropriate form of the words from the dialogue.

1 Suzy __has__ __to__ post some letters and send a fax. She ________ leave the office early ________ ________ ________ meet Dave at six. If she ________ the fax to the Grosvenor Express office, she ________ ________ late for her appointment with Dave.

2 Geoffrey always calls Grosvenor Express when he ________ ________ ________ an urgent message. Suzy ________ ________ they had messengers.

3 Suzy ________ ________ the letters to the post office and Mrs Walton ________ ________ Grosvenor Express. Suzy will ________ ____ hurry ________ the post office closes in ten minutes.

4 Suzy is back from the post office. She was quick ________ she ________ ________ ________ ________.

5 Simon ________ ________ the Grosvenor Express office. He'll ________ ________ ________ the fax.

Compare these sentences.

1 Children in England have to go to school until they are sixteen.
2 I must get my hair cut. It's too long.
3 I'll have to catch the 10.30 train.
4 You really must visit your mother-in-law.
5 You'll have to hurry. You'll miss the bus.

Rule: 'Have to' and ________ have similar meanings. They both indicate an obligation to do something.

Exercise 2

Match the lines in A with the lines in B and join them with 'in order to' or 'because.'

A

1 Suzy will have to go to the post office .....
2 I'll have to hurry .....
3 Suzy will have to tidy the office .....
4 You must write to your mother .....
5 We'll have to phone the travel agency .....
6 I must leave my flat at 9 o'clock in the morning .....

B

a) ..... my favourite television programme starts in half an hour.
b) ..... she's worried about you.
c) ..... someone important is coming tomorrow.
d) ..... be at work by 10 o'clock.
e) ..... post Geoffrey's letters.
f) ..... book our plane tickets.

Exercise 3

Practise this dialogue with your partner. Take turns to be A and B.

A: Why must you (1) rush?
B: I have to (2) catch the early train.
A: Why must you (3) go by train?
B: In order to (4) arrive on time.
A: Don't worry! I'll lend you my (5) car.
B: Thanks a million. I'll really take care of (6) it.

(1) wear those clothes; read that book; make a phone call

(2) go to a job interview; study for my exam; speak to Bill

(3) get a new job; take an exam; contact him

(4) earn more money; get a place at university; borrow some records for the party

(5) best suit; lecture notes; tapes

(6) them

Exercise 4

Write on a piece of paper the job you would most like to have and the job you would least like to have. Give the piece of paper to your partner.

When your partner gives you his/her piece of paper, choose one of the jobs and write a description of it.
Write sentences like this:

You'll have to type a lot of letters. You'll have to make cups of tea because . . .

LESSON 36

This Boat Is Being Commandeered

Exercise 1

Answer the following questions.

1 Why do the men say 'customs officers'?
2 Why do the men need a boat?
3 Why doesn't Jack try to stop the men?
4 Why does the man say 'Go ahead' to Yolanda?
5 Does Jack think the government will win?
6 What is the leader's name?
7 Why is Yolanda pleased?

Exercise 2

Study the sentences and complete the rule.

'This boat is being commandeered.'
'We're being helped.'

Rule: the Present Continuous Passive consists of three parts:
(i) the correct person of the verb ________ (eg *is, are*)
(ii) the present participle 'being'
(iii) the ________ participle (eg *helped*)

Complete the table with the Present Continuous Passive of 'to help'.

I am being helped	We ________
You are ________	You ________
He is ________	They ________
She ________	
It ________	

Interrogative: *Am I being helped?* Etc.
Negative: *I am not being helped.* Etc.
(spoken: *I'm not being helped.*)

Complete the paragraph, using the Present Continuous Passive.

The natural world (1) ________ (destroy) these days. Many forests (2) ________ (cut down) and large areas (3) ________ (turn) into deserts by modern farming methods. The sea (4) ________ (pollute) more and more by industrial waste. The atmosphere (5) ________ (destroy) by chemicals. Birds and animals (6) ________ (kill) and many species are extinct.

Exercise 3

'Every islander used to have a little land.'

Remember that 'used to' refers to a continuous state or repeated events in a past period.

Interrogative (normally):	Did I use to . . . . . ? (Did you use to . . . etc.)
Negative (normally):	I didn't use to . . . . . (You didn't use to . . . etc.)
Negative Interrogative:	Didn't I use to . . . . . ? (Didn't you use to . . . etc.)

Fill in the blanks with 'used to' + verb. Choose the verbs from the list below.

The crew of the *Ocean Explorer* are now working together to raise money for the Institute, but in the past they (1) ________ many different things. Lisa (2) ________ to school in Holland. Yolanda (3) ________ photographs for a fashion magazine. Jack always worked at sea, but he (4) ________ on merchant ships. Rob (5) ________ a radio operator on an oil rig. On the other hand, Howard never worked near the sea. He (6) ________ a large forest in the north of England. As for Meg, she (7) ________ research projects at the Ocean Institute.

Verbs: to go; to work; to do; to take; to direct; to manage; to be

Exercise 4

Find words in the cartoon with the following meanings.

1 rather, a bit pre________
2 a type of fast boat a la________
3 people who import things without paying tax sm________
4 men who check imports and collect tax cu________ off________
5 a person who lives on an island an is________

Exercise 5

Write at least five sentences about the things that are being done in all or any of the following:

your work, your house, your town, your country.
(Use the Present Continuous Passive!)

LESSON 37

Everyone's a Big Happy Family Down Under

Now in Auckland, New Zealand, the team are learning about life Down Under.

Lisa Jack, I can't see Meg anywhere.
Jack Well, she must be somewhere.
Lisa But I've looked everywhere for her.
Jack Look, she's sitting over there, and there's someone with her.
Lisa Who is she talking to? I don't know him.
Jack Let's go over and speak to them.

They walk over to Meg's table.

Jack Hi, Meg. Can we join you?
Meg With pleasure. I'd like to introduce you to our contact, Koro Hohepa. Koro, meet two of the crew: Lisa Anders and Jack Craig.
Koro Hello. And welcome to Aotearoa – that's our Maori name for New Zealand. Where are you from, Jack?
Jack Sydney.
Koro Oh, a neighbour. Well, Sydney's a great place.
Meg It's rather like Auckland, I think. There's a superb harbour and a big bridge. And there are fabulous beaches everywhere.
Jack Yeah, but only Sydney's got an opera house.
Koro True, but there are sharks everywhere. And not just in the water.
Jack Yeah. Like those ones in Tobanau.
Lisa What did you say that for, Jack? The Tobanau people were great.
Koro Yes, but there's some trouble there now, isn't there? Anyway, I'm not really serious. We Kiwis and Aussies make fun of each other, you know.
Lisa Like brothers.
Koro That's right. Everyone's a big, happy family Down Under. Where are you from, Lisa?
Lisa From Holland. From Zeeland, in fact.
Jack Ah, so you're from old Zeeland, and now you're in New Zealand.
Lisa No, Jack, I'm in Aotearoa now.

Exercise 1

Answer the following questions.

1 'Down Under' refers to
  a) Latin America.
  b) the Antarctic.
  c) Australia and New Zealand.
  d) the Southern Hemisphere.

2 'Aotearoa' is the ________ name for ________.

3 What three things have Sydney and Auckland got in common?
____
____
____

4 What does Koro mean when he says that sharks are 'not just in the water'?

5 Aussies = Australians
Kiwis = ________

6 From which part of the Netherlands does the English name for Aotearoa come from?

Exercise 2

Study these sentences and complete the rule.

I can't see her *anywhere.*
Have you seen her *anywhere?*
She must be *somewhere.*
She's sitting with *someone.*
I haven't seen *anyone.*
Have you seen *anyone?*

Rule: We use 'somewhere' with affirmative statements. We use '________' with negative statements and with ________. We use 'someone' with ________ statements and we use 'anyone' with ________ and with questions.

Complete these sentences with 'somewhere , anywhere, someone, anyone'.

1 Lisa looked everywhere but she couldn't see Meg ________.
2 Jack noticed Meg sitting with ________.
3 Have you seen my bike ________?
4 ________ has borrowed it.
5 I didn't see ________ take it.
6 I've searched ________ and I can't see it ________.
7 Let's go ________ interesting this weekend.

Exercise 3

Practise this dialogue. Take turns to be A and B.

A: What are you looking for?
B: I've left (1) my pen somewhere, and now I can't find (2) it.
A: Have you looked everywhere?
B: Yes, I have. I've looked for (2) it (3) in the study and in the living room. Everywhere, in fact.
A: Have you looked (4) in the kitchen?
B: No, I haven't.
A: Well, I'm sure you'll find (2) it there.

(1) my trainers; my cassettes; my walkman*

(2) them

(3) in the hall; in my bedroom; on the balcony*

(4) in the dining room; in the lounge; in the bathroom

* Add your own information.

Exercise 4

Write a brief description of a town or city, but without giving the name. Collect the descriptions and read them aloud. Try to guess the name of the place.

Example:

This city is somewhere in Latin America. It has beautiful beaches, high hills and a large statue of Christ.
Answer: *Rio de Janeiro.*

LESSON 38

They Were Getting Their Revenge

Yolanda and Rob have been sightseeing and they report their travels to Lisa and Jack.

Lisa Where have you two been?
Robert To Rotorua.
Jack The place with the thermal activity?
Yolanda Yeah, that's right. It's like Yellowstone Park in the States.
Robert We rented a car yesterday. Then we drove to a town called Hamilton. It's on the Waikato River. It's a very nice place. We had lunch there – a real New Zealand meal: roast lamb, mint sauce, roast potatoes, green peas. And then we had Pavlova – it's the national dessert.
Lisa It sounds like a real English meal to me.
Yolanda Yeah, that's what I said to the waitress. But she said that roast lamb and Pavlova are 'the quintessential New Zealand meal'.
Lisa What did she mean by that?
Yolanda I guess she meant that it was the most typical and authentic New Zealand meal. After all, there are more sheep and cattle than people here.
Robert The Pavlova was decorated with cream – and kiwi fruit.
Yolanda Anyway, after we had finished our quintessential meal, we continued south to Rotorua.
Robert It's a fascinating place. We visited the boiling mud pools and we saw the geysers, and after that, we ate some Maori food cooked in a *haangi*.
Lisa A what?
Robert Oh, it's an earth oven. First, they put very hot stones in a hole in the ground, the food is put onto the stones, and then the whole lot is covered with leaves and earth. It's a traditional Polynesian way of cooking.
Yolanda The food has a unique taste – kind of smoked. There were sweet potatoes and roast pig. Then we visited a Maori *pa* – that's Maori for village – where we saw some Maori dancing.
Jack Did you see a *haka*?
Yolanda Their war dance? We sure did. But then, Rob began to feel ill.
Lisa Oh, that's too bad.
Jack I reckon the lamb and the pig were getting their revenge.

Rotorua, New Zealand

Exercise 1

Answer the following:

1 Name two places visited by Yolanda and Rob.
2 Write down their lunch menu.
3 'Quintessential' means ________.
4 Sheep and cattle outnumber people in New Zealand. True or false?
5 What is a *haangi* used for?
6 What did the Maori food taste like?

Exercise 2

Here are the names of the main parts of a meal.

Words used on a menu	Words people often say
hors d'oeuvres	starters
soup	soup
entree	main course
dessert	sweet, pudding, afters

What is the 'quintessential' meal in your country? Discuss this and write a menu of a typical meal.

Exercise 3

Yolanda took some photographs showing how a *haangi* is made. Here are the captions for her photographs in muddled order. Put them in the correct sequence and add some sequencers – *next, after that, finally* – to show the order of steps.

The *haangi* is covered with leaves and earth.
Stones are placed on the wood.
A hole is dug in the ground.
When the stones are hot, the wood is removed.
After two hours, the *haangi* is uncovered.
Food is prepared and wrapped in leaves.
Firewood is put in the hole.
A fire is lit.
The wrapped food is placed on the stones.

Exercise 4

A *haangi* is quintessentially Polynesian. Write a description of how something similar is made or done in your country. It could be preparing a feast or festival or making something. Use the Present Passive voice, like the description in Exercise 3, and sequencers to show the order of steps.

LESSON 39

I'd Rather Be Sure Than Sorry

Back at the Ocean Institute, Suzy is booking a flight to Australia for Geoffrey.

Telephonist Landfall Travel. Melanie speaking. Can I help you?
Suzy Yes, I want to make bookings for Australia. My boss has to be in Sydney on Friday week.
Clerk I see. That doesn't give us much time. I can only offer you Club or First Class.
Suzy That's all right. You'd better book him on whatever is available.
Clerk Well, let's have a look. I can offer you flights from Heathrow via Singapore, Bangkok, or Colombo, with stop-overs depending on the route.
Suzy And all of these go to Sydney?
Clerk Yes, they do. But the Colombo flight goes to Perth first. That's in Western Australia.
Suzy I see. I'd better ask him first. Can I call you back?
Clerk Certainly. Ask for Dick.

Later that day.

Suzy So those are the choices, Geoff.
Geoff As it's costing a lot, I'd rather make the best use of the money. I've got to be in Sydney for the fifteenth. So, if I leave the day after tomorrow, I can spend about six days on the journey and visit Singapore and Perth.
Suzy That'll give you time to go to both, but you'd better give yourself some time to recover from jet lag.
Geoff No problem. I'm travelling first class and I'd sooner sleep on the plane than on the ground.
Suzy OK, I'll call the agent and ask if you can take that route.
Geoff And check on visa requirements, will you? I think I'll need a visa for Australia.
Suzy Are you sure?
Geoff No, I'm not sure. But I'd rather be sure than sorry.

Exercise 1

Complete the following table.

1 Classes available to Australia.

Tourist	Club	First

2 Routes available to Sydney. Which are the ones listed by the travel agent?
Bahrain, Bangkok, Colombo, Dubai, Hong Kong, Perth, Singapore, Seychelles, Zurich

3 Complete this itinerary for Geoff's journey.

Place	Activity	Date	Day
London	making arrangements		
	departing		Sunday
Sydney		15th	

4 Why would Geoff rather be sure than sorry?

Exercise 2

When speaking, people say ''d' for 'would', and 'had'.

Example:

You'd better book him on whatever flight is available. (You had better)
I'd rather make the best use of the money. (I would rather)

Rule: We use '________' + 'better' + verb to make a recommendation to ourselves or to others.

We use '________' + 'rather' + verb to express a preference.

Complete the sentences below. Some make recommendations, some express a preference.

Example:

Geoff's travelling on the non-stop flight. I/have a stop over.
I'd rather have a stop over.

1 I'm going to Milan next weekend. I/go to Turin.
2 Lisa's driving to Alice Springs. She/carry plenty of water.
3 Meg's going swimming in the harbour. She/watch out for sharks.
4 Yolanda's going to the opera. Rob/go to the jazz concert.
5 Jack is going to the pub. I/go to a wine bar.
6 Jack is seeing two different girls. He/take care.
7 Geoff is flying BA. I/fly Quantas.
8 Howard won't go swimming in the harbour. He/be sure than sorry.

Exercise 3

Practise this dialogue with a partner. Take turns to be A and B.

A: Where shall we go this weekend?
B: I'd like to go to (1) the beach.
A: I'd rather go to (2) the countryside.
B: Can we go to the (1) beach on Saturday and (2) the countryside on Sunday instead?
A: We'd better not.
B: Why?
A: Because we'd better (3) work in the garden.

(1) the Henley Regatta; the Picasso exhibition; the races*

(2) the motor show; the jazz festival; the dog show*

(3) clean the kitchen; paint the sitting room; repair the car*

* Use your own information.

Exercise 4

What are you going to do
on Friday night?
next weekend?
for your next vacation?
next year?

What would you rather do
on Friday night?
next weekend?
for your next vacation?
next year?

Find someone in the class who would rather do the same things as you.

LESSON 40

I'd Have Helped Them

Exercise 1

Choose True or False. Then write the sentences in the text that give the answers.

1 Meg is going to see Geoffrey at the party.
2 Lisa didn't like the men from Tobanau.
3 Meg decides to say goodnight to everybody.
4 Yolanda feels very tired.
5 Meg doesn't know where Geoff and Jack are.
6 Jack has broken a bone in his foot.

Exercise 2

Jack *If I had seen her, I would have asked* her to join us.
('If *I'd seen* her, *I'd have asked* her to join us.')
Did Jack see Meg? No. Did he ask her? No.

Study the forms of the verb used in this type of 'If' sentence. The forms are the same for all persons, so we say:

I/you/he/she/it/we/they had seen (had = *'d* in spoken English)
Negative: I had not seen (I hadn't seen)

I/you/he/she/it/we/they would have asked (would = *'d* in speech after the subject)
Negative: I would not have asked (I wouldn't have asked)

Interrogative: *Would I have asked?*
Negative Interrogative: *Wouldn't I have asked?*

Put the verb in the correct place and the correct form.

1 If we ________ those men, they ________ us. (not help) (shoot)
2 If the men ________ Lisa, she ________ them. (keep) (help)
3 If Jack ________ Meg, he ________ her to join them. (ask) (see)
4 If the taxi ________ an accident, Geoff ________ his foot. (not have) (not break)
5 The accident ________, if Jack and Geoff ________ back with Meg. (not happen) (go)
6 They ________ tired, if they ________ to bed early. (not be) (go)
7 They ________, themselves if they ________ at home. (not enjoy) (stay)
8 They ________ the diamonds if there ________ a storm. (not find) (not be)

Exercise 3

Study the dialogue and in pairs make up similar dialogues. Take turns to be A and B.

A: What would you have done if you hadn't (1) joined the police?
B: I'd probably have (2) joined the army.
A: Oh, you'd have made a good (3) soldier.
B: Do you really think so?
A: Yes, of course.

(1) joined the church; gone on the stage; joined the bank; gone into computers

(2) gone into education; gone into Parliament; worked for a newspaper; gone into medicine

(3) teacher; politician; journalist; doctor

Exercise 4

Think about some events in your life. Write what would (or would not) have happened, if you had (or had not) done certain things. eg

I wouldn't have met my husband/wife, if I hadn't gone to University.
I would have bought a house when I was young, if I had had enough money.

LESSON 41

So Is Mine!

Stella works at the hospital in Sydney where Geoffrey is recovering from his accident. It's lunch time and Stella is in the park outside the hospital.

Stella Is this seat taken?
Kylie No, make yourself comfortable. I'm going in a minute anyway. I'm just waiting for a friend.
Stella Well, in that case I'll sit here and eat my sandwiches. It's such a fantastic day. It's a pity to sit inside an office.
Kylie Oh, do you work in that bank across the road?
Stella No, actually I work in the hospital.
Kylie Do you? So do I. Which part?
Stella Administration. What about you?
Kylie I'm a nurse. I work on the wards.
Stella I bet that's a difficult job. Do you enjoy it?
Kylie Yes, I do. It's hard work, but I meet lots of interesting people. In fact I met my boyfriend at the hospital.
Stella Yes, so did I . . . . . and so did most of the girls in my department. Was your boyfriend a patient?
Kylie He was admitted for a few hours overnight. He had a slight accident, you see. But I met him when he was visiting a friend.
Stella So did I. I mean . . . . . I met my boyfriend when he came to see someone in hospital. Isn't that funny? Actually I haven't known my boyfriend long.
Kylie No, neither have I. Just a few days. He doesn't live here in Sydney. He's just passing through.
Stella Really! So is mine. What a coincidence! Is he from Europe or something?
Kylie No, he's Australian. He's from Sydney.
Stella So is mine! He's a sailor.
Kylie Goodness! Mine's a yachtsman.
Stella Well, they say everyone loves a sailor.
Kylie Unfortunately my sailor is late. I'm never late for my dates.
Stella No, neither am I.
Kylie If he doesn't arrive in ten minutes, I'm having lunch without him.
Stella Poor chap. He's really in trouble. What's his name?
Kylie Jack.
Stella You're kidding! What does he look like?
Kylie See for yourself. Here he comes.
Jack Hi there, Kylie.
Stella Hello, Jack.
Jack Stella! What are you doing here?
Stella I'm glad that you're here, Jack. I've got a few questions to ask you.
Kylie And so have I.

Exercise 1

Answer the following questions.

1 Where is Stella?
2 Where does Kylie work and what does she do?
3 Why does Kylie like her job?
4 Who did Kylie meet at the hospital?
5 Why was Stella's boyfriend at the hospital?
6 Where is Kylie's boyfriend from?
7 What does Stella's boyfriend do?
8 What will happen if Kylie's boyfriend doesn't arrive in ten minutes?

Exercise 2

Here are parts of the conversation between Stella and Kylie. Match them correctly.

A

1 I work in the hospital.
2 I met my boyfriend at the hospital.
3 I'm never late for my dates.
4 I've got a few questions to ask you.
5 I haven't known my boyfriend long.
6 He's just passing through.

B

a) Neither am I.
b) So is mine.
c) So have I.
d) So do I.
e) So did I.
f) Neither have I.

Exercise 3

Notice how we agree with an affirmative sentence:

1 I'm (am) a nurse. → So am I (are you, etc)
2 I've seen the film. → So have I (have you, has he, etc)
3 I can see the office. → So can I (can you, etc)
But:
4 I live in the town. So do I (do you, does he, etc)
5 I lived in the town. So did I (did you, etc)

This is how we agree with a negative sentence:

1 I'm not a driver. Neither am I.
2 I haven't read it. Neither have I.
3 I can't see the boat. Neither can I.
But:
4 I don't live in the town. Neither do I.
5 I didn't live in the town. Neither did I.

Jane and Sally are having lunch together. What does Sally say?

Jane I'm a friend of Harrison Ford.
Sally Really! So ________
Jane I've already seen his latest film.
Sally Yes, so ________
Jane Actually I met Harrison for dinner last week.
Sally What a coincidence! So ________
Jane There's so much to talk about. I'm glad that you're here.
Sally So ________
Jane I'd pay the bill, but I haven't got my cheque book with me.
Sally Neither ________

Practise this dialogue with your partner and invent other dialogues.

Exercise 4

A very important person is visiting your town. You have to show him/her around, but you don't know anything about the visitor's likes and dislikes. Say who the visitor is. Make plans for his/her visit. Write sentences like this:

On Monday if everything goes according to plan, I'm meeting ________.
If she/he is hungry, I'm taking her/him. . . . .

LESSON 42

Too Spicey for the Average Tourist

Monday 7.30pm

Lost and found in the Indian Ocean
By Antonia Harte

I came here in search of the *Ocean Explorer*, and I found an unexplored world. I'm in Madagascar – the fourth largest island in the world. It is too unsophisticated for ordinary tourists to visit. In fact, it is not easy to visit Madagascar.

Accommodation here is a problem. The local guest houses are far too old and lack basic facilities; the few modern hotels are far too ugly and much too expensive. I chose a small farm instead.

My first shopping expedition was a new experience: in Madagascar shopping and sightseeing are inseparable. There are many attractive handicrafts to buy: carved wooden bowls, leather goods, traditional jewellery, vividly coloured cloth, and a wide variety of ceramics and earthenware. If you want to buy something, you have to bargain.

In the village of Ivontaka I tried the local delicacies: foods that are too spicey for the average tourist; rice dishes that taste sublime; unidentifiable fruits that look enticing and smell curious. I saw some of the island's famous lemurs. These black-faced creatures are primates only found in Madagascar. From a distance they look human and you feel uneasy when they stare at you.

With my guide, I explored the local nature reserve. The earth smelt fresh and sweet after the November rains. The Malagasy people have replaced half of their island's forests with poor-quality cropland and now rivers are drying up in the south. Here in the north the remaining rain forests look and sound mysterious.

In Monday night's programme I'll consider how tourism can help this island and I'll explain why Madagascar is much too precious to lose.

Exercise 1

Read the text and choose the best ending for each sentence.

1 Antonia Harte is writing about
  a) a new adventure film.
  b) her latest book.
  c) a television programme.
2 Antonia stayed at a
  a) local guest house.
  b) small farm.
  c) modern hotel.
3 On her first shopping expedition, Antonia
  a) bought some carved wooden bowls.
  b) wanted to buy something.
  c) had a new experience.
4 Lemurs are
  a) local delicacies.
  b) primates.
  c) a type of fruit.
5 Antonia visited the
  a) west.
  b) north.
  c) south.

Exercise 2

Read the article and then write the missing information in the table.

1	The rain forests ________	look ________	mysterious ________
2	________	________	mysterious ________
3	________	taste ________	________
4	Fruits ________	________	enticing ________
5	________	feel ________	________
6	The earth ________	________	fresh ________
7	________	________	human ________
8	________	smelt ________	________
9	________	________	curious ________

Rule We can use verbs such as 'look', 'smell', 'feel', 'taste', and 'sound' followed by an adjective, eg mysterious.

Exercise 3

Read this conversation between Phil and David. Fill the (A) spaces with 'far too' or 'much too' + adjective.
Fill the (B) spaces with 'to' + verb.
Choose from these words:

A: salty/expensive/cold/strong
B: to stay/to wear/to drink/to eat

Phil What was the weather like in Scotland?
David The climate was a problem. It was (A) ________ for me (B) ________ my cotton jacket.
Phil Did you like the local Scottish delicacies?
David No, I'm afraid the food was a problem too. It was (A) ________ for me (B) ________.
Phil What about the whisky?
David I didn't like it at all. It was (A) ________ for me (B) ________.
Phil You stayed at a hotel in Edinburgh, didn't you? Did you stay long?
David No, it was (A) ________ for me (B) ________ there. It's not easy to visit Scotland.

Practise the dialogue with your partner. Invent other dialogues about another country.

Exercise 4

Last night you had a meal in a top-class restaurant. The food was terrible. Write a letter of complaint to the Restaurant Manager. Start your letter like this:

Dear Sir,
Last night I ate in your restaurant. I'm sorry to say that the food tasted . . . . .

Continue by writing about:

the smell of the fish
the colour of the vegetables
the appearance of the potatoes
the taste of the wine

Say why you couldn't eat certain foods. Perhaps they were

too hot?
too cold?
too sweet?
too salty?

End your letter like this:

I would like a full refund. I think it is only fair for you to do so.
I look forward to hearing from you soon,
Yours faithfully,

Did You Pick the Brochures up?

Madagascar

Suzy Have you got the brochures?
Dave What?
Suzy The brochures from the travel agent. Did you pick them up?
Dave I can't hear you.
Suzy Why don't you switch your Walkman off?
Dave What did you say?
Suzy Dave, will you please turn off your Walkman and take those headphones off.
Dave Sorry, Suzy.
Suzy That's better. Now, did you pick the brochures up from the travel agency?
Dave Yes, I did, but I left them at home.
Suzy At home? They're no use to me there, are they? I phoned up the travel agent specially and asked him to keep those brochures for me, and now you've forgotten them.
Dave I'll bring them in tomorrow.
Suzy I want them today. It's November, Dave. My holiday's in January. If we want to go on holiday together, we'll have to make some decisions right away. If we don't book now, it'll be too late.
Dave Oh dear, it sounds like a matter of life and death. Why don't we just stay with my sister? She can put us up.
Suzy Although I like your sister very much, Dave, I really don't want to go to Brighton again for my holidays. I want to go to somewhere exciting like . . . like Madagascar.
Dave You always want to go where the *Ocean Explorer* goes. Yesterday you were mad about Rio and now it's Madagascar. If the *Ocean Explorer* goes to Siberia, you'll want to go there too.
Suzy How did you know that?
Dave What? About Siberia?
Suzy How did you know that the *Ocean Explorer* was in Madagascar?
Dave I knew because Simon told me.
Suzy And just how did he find that out? Your friend Simon knows too much. I don't like him. He looks shifty and to be honest, Dave, he gives me the creeps.

Exercise 1

Read the dialogue and answer the questions.

1 Why can't Dave hear Suzy?
2 What did Dave leave at home?
3 Who did Suzy phone up?
4 When is Suzy's holiday?
5 What will happen if Dave and Suzy don't book their holiday now?
6 Who lives in Brighton?
7 Where does Suzy want to go for her holidays?
8 What did Simon tell Dave?
9 Why doesn't Suzy like Simon?

Exercise 2

Rule: Study this example.

Verb	Object	Particle
Did you phone	him	up?

A phrasal verb is a verb + a particle.

Read the dialogue again and fill in the missing words.

1 Did you ________ them ________?
2 She can ________ us ________.
3 I'll ________ them ________ tomorrow.
4 ________ those headphones ________.
5 Why don't you ________ your Walkman ________?
6 How did he ________ that ________?
7 Please ________ ________ your Walkman.
8 I ________ ________ the travel agent.

Exercise 3

The words and phrases in A are in the dialogue. Match them with the definitions in B.

A

1 gives me the creeps
2 find out
3 pick (them) up
4 right away
5 looks shifty
6 mad
7 put (us) up
8 a matter of life and death

B

a) extremely important
b) has a suspicious appearance
c) makes me feel uncomfortable
d) very enthusiastic
e) provide somewhere to stay
f) collect something
g) immediately
h) get some information

Exercise 4

Join these sentences with 'although' or 'because'.

1 I don't want to spend my holiday with her. I like your sister.

Although I like your sister, I don't want to spend my holiday with her.

2 I left them at home. I haven't got the brochures.
3 He looks shifty. I don't like him.
4 I have a good job. I don't earn much money.
5 Our holiday is in July. We have to book our plane seats in February.
6 It's too expensive. I can't go on holiday to Madagascar.

Write the sentences in the dialogue below, and then practise the dialogue with a partner.

Steven Why don't we stay with my sister for our holidays?
Ann ________________________________
____
Steven We can stay with my friend George in Blackpool.
Ann ________________________________
Steven Well, we'll wait until the summer and we'll book a holiday abroad.
Ann ________________________________
____
Let's look at the brochures now.
Steven ________________________________
Ann I've already picked a holiday. I want to go to Madagascar.
Steven ________________________________
Ann Nonsense. Anyway, you've got lots of money.
Steven ________________________________
____

Exercise 5

Write a short description of what you plan to do tomorrow. Use at least five of these phrasal verbs.

take back	try on	put up
put on	find out	phone up
pick up	switch on	
fill in	turn off	

Begin like this:

I've got a lot to do tomorrow. First of all I'll . . . . .

I Can't Find Anything

Exercise 1

Put the following sentences in order according to the text.

a) The frogman went onto the boat. ____
b) Yolanda went on deck in her new outfit. ____
c) A frogman started to swim to the *Ocean Explorer*. __1__
d) Everyone admired it. ____
e) Jack tried to capture the frogman. ____
f) Jack decided to stay on the boat. ____
g) He escaped. ____
h) They left Jack on the boat. ____

Exercise 2

Complete the tables.

-one
I met *someone*.
I met *no one*.
I didn't meet *anyone*.
Did you meet *anyone*?
I met *everyone*.

-thing
I can see ________*thing*.
I can see *nothing*.
I can't see ________.
Can you see ________?
I can see *everything*.

-where
I'm going *somewhere*.
I'm going ________*where*.
I'm not going ________
Are you going ________?
I'm going ________.

Exercise 3

Reorder the letters to make a word that appears in the text. Some phrases are given to help you.

1 sirrange – something to wear in your ears
2 rimor – something to look at when you brush your hair
3 rimana – somewhere to keep boats
4 oocca – something to drink
5 gramnof – someone who can swim under the water

Exercise 4

Look at the example and complete the rule.

(Frame 2) **Meg** We should leave.
(Frame 5) **Howard** We must leave!

Rule

Quite strong (obligation)	Very strong (necessity)
We use: ________.	We use: ________

Complete the following sentences (in some cases both are possible).

1 You're driving a car. The traffic lights turn red. You ________ stop.
2 You're sitting in a bus which is full. A lady with a baby comes on. You ________ offer her your seat.
3 If you want to study the history of art, you ________ learn Italian.
4 If you want to communicate with everyone in Italy you ________ learn Italian.
5 If people want to travel to the USA, they ________ have a valid passport.
6 If you want to drive a car in England, you ________ be 17.
7 In Britain, you ________ go to school till you are sixteen.
8 People ________ not eat too much sugar.
9 On the London underground, you ________ not smoke.
10 If you want to be healthy, you ________ not smoke.

Exercise 5

Imagine you are the family friend of a young person who is leaving home to work in a large city abroad. Write a brief letter, telling him/her what he/she should do, and must do.

LESSON 45

Either You Pay, Or We Stay

The expedition is in Lagos, and Howard is having problems with supplies.

Lisa What's the matter, Howard?

Howard Supplies. It's the supplies. Especially the diesel fuel. We have a service shortage.

Lisa What do you mean?

Howard Well, when we arrived, Jack told me to go to Sea Supplies. So, I went to them and they promised to deliver the supplies within two days. That was four days ago.

Lisa Have you spoken to them about it?

Howard Of course I have. And they promised to look into it. I told them either they delivered by tomorrow, or I would cancel the order.

Lisa Well, here's Jack. Maybe he can help.

Jack Hello, you two. Howard, did you know that no one has delivered the fuel yet? They should've delivered it by now. You did pay 'dash', didn't you, Howard?

Howard What's that? A bribe?

Jack No, not a bribe. You are – how shall I put it? – oiling the wheels. It's a custom. You either pay 'dash' or you get nothing.

Howard But that's crazy, paying someone to do you a service!

Jack Maybe it is crazy. But that's the custom here. Go to the suppliers. Speak to the clerk. Give him some 'dash' – about $20 will be enough – and arrange delivery.

Lisa What do you say in English, Howard? 'When in Rome, do as the Romans do.'

Howard That's all very well, Lisa. But I am not a Roman or a Nigerian.

Jack No, but either you pay, or we stay.

Howard OK, OK. I'll pay.

Exercise 1

1 Put the sentences into the correct sequence.
   a) The supplies were not delivered. ____
   b) Howard went to Sea Supplies. ____
   c) They promised delivery. ____
   d) Four days passed. ____
   e) Jack told Howard to go to Sea Supplies. ____
   f) Sea Supplies promised delivery within two days. ____
   g) The expedition arrived in Lagos. __1__
   h) Howard phoned Sea Supplies. ____

2 Why haven't Sea Supplies delivered the supplies?

3 What should Howard do? Put these in order.
   a) Speak to the clerk.
   b) Visit Sea Supplies.
   c) Pay him a service charge.

4 Jack said, 'Either you pay, or we stay' Pay what? Stay where?

Exercise 2

Here is what people actually said:

'We'll deliver the supplies within two days.'
'We'll look into it.'

Find the parts of the dialogue which report these statements and complete the rule.

Rule: When we report a promise, we use 'promise' + 'to' + verb:
They ________ to ________ the supplies within two days.

Change these to reported promises.

1 **Howard** I'll telephone the suppliers.
2 **Jack** I'll arrange payment.
3 **Geoff** I'll send some more funds.
4 **Howard** I'll call the suppliers.

Compare these two sentences:

Howard promised to telephone the suppliers.
Howard promised Meg that he would telephone the suppliers.

Rule: If the person to whom the promise is made is mentioned, then the pattern is:
Person A promised Person B that . . . .
Report these promises, following the pattern in the second sentence above.

1 **Suppliers to Howard** We'll deliver tomorrow.
2 **Geoff to Meg** I'll transfer funds to Lagos.
3 **Lisa to Jack** I'll cook curry for dinner.
4 **Jack to Lisa** I'll get some lager to drink with the curry.
5 **Rob to Yolanda** I'll take you to a Nigerian pop concert.

Exercise 3

Yolanda and Rob are discussing what to do. They have several choices. Practise their dialogue. Take turns to be A and B. Add choices of your own.

A: What shall we do (1) tonight?
B: I'm not sure. How about (2) going to a concert?
A: Or what about (3) seeing a film?
B: Well, either we (2) go to a concert or we (3) see a film.
A: Can't we do both?
B: No, it's either a (2) concert or a (3) film.
A: Well, why not stay at home?
B: What a good idea!

(1) this weekend

(2) go to a concert; go to a nightclub; visit a Yoruba village; go to the beach

(3) go to the night market; visit the museum; work on the boat

Exercise 4

List places in your country where you could go for a weekend vacation.
Write a short letter to a friend proposing choices for the weekend. Follow this pattern.

Either we go to ________ or we stay in ________.
If we go to ________, we can visit/see ________.
But, if we go there, we can't visit/see ________.

LESSON 46

The Traffic Is Terrifying, But the Place Is Fascinating

Dear Mum,

Tomorrow we arrive in the Canaries, where I'll post this letter. Meanwhile we're having an uneventful voyage - thank goodness - after all the problems we've had elsewhere, including Lagos, our last port of call.

Lagos is the main port for Nigeria, which is a very interesting and captivating - and sometimes infuriating - country. For instance, we were delayed there because Howard hadn't paid dash - a kind of 'service charge' (we'd call it a bribe) for the delivery of fuel. He ordered fuel as soon as we had arrived. Then days passed, and no supplies were delivered. Eventually, dash was paid - and suddenly, everything we had ordered was delivered. We were charged the agreed price, so everything was alright.

The voyage out of Lagos has been trouble-free, although the West African coast is tricky. I can see why it was avoided by the early navigators. Meanwhile, our life aboard ship continues as usual. We each take a turn on the watch, ie. on duty. Sometimes I share the watch with Yolanda - she's the American. She found Nigeria very interesting because she is black. She says that although her ancestors came from West Africa, she doesn't feel West African and that at heart she is an American. But, she thinks that Nigerian culture is very exciting. So do I.

They have some really great musicians there. Yolanda and I went to a concert by one of their top groups. It was led by Sonny Madolo, and the concert was really exciting. There was so much energy and sound and movement. It was a new world of music. I want to hear more of it.

Lagos itself is rather disappointing and the traffic is terrifying, and I was almost killed several times. We hired a car and Yolanda drove. Mind you, her driving is pretty terrifying, too. She drove like a formula 1 driver.

We visited some places near Lagos. One day we went to a Yoruba cult house. I can now see a connection with Macumba and Condomble in Brazil because, of course, the slaves who were taken to Brazil in the early days were from West Africa. Many of the deities in the cult house were similar to the ones we saw in the Brazilian Macumba church. Fascinating!

Well, I'll finish this now.

Love,
Robert.

Exercise 1

Choose True or False. Then write the sentences which give you the answers.

1 They paid the agreed price for supplies.
2 The voyage from Lagos has had problems.
3 The West African coast is dangerous.
4 Early explorers didn't go along the West African coast.
5 Yolanda thinks that she is an African.
6 Rob didn't find Sonny Madolo's music very exciting.
7 Slaves from West Africa took their religion to Brazil.

Exercise 2

Pattern: I found X very *-ing* because it is so ________.

Example: I found Nigeria very interesting because it is so full of exciting things.

Adjectives:

Negative	**Positive**
disappointing	captivating
infuriating	exciting
terrifying	fascinating
	interesting

Complete the sentences with an adjective from the list, and the reason from the text.

1 Rob found Nigeria ________ because they had to pay dash.
2 Yolanda found Nigeria ________ because ________.
3 Rob thought the concert was ________ because ________.
4 Rob said that the traffic was ________ because ________.
5 Rob found Yolanda's driving ________ because ________.
6 Rob found the Yoruba cult house ________ because ________.

Now write two similar sentences about places or events which you know.

Exercise 3

Practise this dialogue with a partner. Take turns to be A and B.

A: Where did you go for your vacation?
B: To (1) the Yemen.
A: How (2) interesting.
B: (3) Well, it wasn't really very interesting.
A: (4) Didn't you visit the Marib Dam?
B: Yes, (5) but we had problems with our travel permit. It was quite infuriating.
A: (6) Oh, I'm very sorry you were disappointed.

(1) India; Brazil; Kenya

(2) exciting; fascinating

(3) a) Well, it wasn't really very interesting/exciting/fascinating.
b) Yes, it was very interesting/exciting/fascinating.

(4) a) Didn't you see the Taj Mahal? Didn't you visit the Iguassu Falls? Didn't you go to a game reserve?
b) Did you see the Taj Mahal? Did you visit the Iguassu Falls? Did you go to a game reserve?

(5) a) but I wasn't feeling very well when we were there. It was most upsetting.; but the weather wasn't very good when we were there. It was most disappointing.; but our Landcruiser broke down. It was most infuriating.
b) we saw it by moonlight. It was quite enchanting; we stayed at an excellent hotel. It was very relaxing; we saw lots of wild animals. It was really exciting.

(6) I'm so glad you enjoyed yourself.

Exercise 4

Have you been on a holiday that was (a) very interesting or exciting, or (b) very disappointing? Write a 'postcard' to your partner about this holiday. Exchange postcards and write a suitable, short reply to your partner. Use the language from Exercises 2 and 3.

LESSON 47

They Must Be Eliminated!

In London, Otto Bergman and one of his aides discuss where the expedition is and plan their revenge.

Otto Bergman What's the latest news?
Aide They went to Lagos. Simon Dean gave me a copy of a telex from there.
Otto Yes, yes, we knew about that long ago. Did they collect any diamonds there?
Aide We don't know, boss.
Otto That's not good enough! Something must be done as soon as possible to find out.
Aide Yes, boss. But we think they did. Anyway, one thing's for sure – they've just left the Canaries. Simon called me. Walton had a phone call from the Brooke woman. Simon said that they're heading for Portugal.
Otto When will they arrive there?
Aide Tuesday or Wednesday at the latest.
Otto Right. We must take action. Have you been in touch with Jim Winstanley? He's expensive, but he's the best man for the job.
Aide No, not yet.
Otto Idiot! Get him out to Lisbon at once. They must be stopped before they reach England.
Aide Yeah, but how and when, boss?
Otto I don't know, but the boat must be sunk.
Aide Where? In the harbour?
Otto No, at sea. In the Bay of Biscay.
Aide At sea. That's difficult. It's easier when they're in a harbour.
Otto Maybe, but it's not impossible. Mr Walton and his yachting friends will be taught a lesson. No one can steal from us.
Aide OK, boss. I'll contact Winstanley immediately.
Otto Tell him I want no mistakes this time. The boat and her crew must be eliminated!

Exercise 1

Answer the following questions.

1 Say whether Otto and his aide are sure or not sure of these things. Copy the part of the dialogue that helps you.

    The expedition went to Lagos.
    They collected some diamonds in Lagos.
    They have left the Canaries.
    Their next stop is in Portugal.
    Winstanley is available.
    The boat will be sunk at sea.

2 What is 'the job'?
3 What will happen to the boat if 'there are no mistakes this time'?

Exercise 2

Find all the verbs of this pattern in the dialogue.

Modal verb + 'be' + past participle

Example: *must be eliminated*

The modal passive consists of ________ parts: modal verb + 'be' + past participle. The modal verb shows the attitude of the speaker to the action.

Match Part A and Part B of these sentences.

Part A	**Part B**
Jackets	must be obtained.
Care	must be eliminated.
A visa	must be worn.
Problems	must be taken.

Exercise 3

The table below shows requirements for British citizens travelling to these countries.

Country	Passport	Visa	Vaccinations
Australia	Yes	Yes	No
Brazil	Yes	No	No
Côte d'Ivoire	Yes	No	Yes
France	Yes	No	No
India	Yes	Yes	Yes
USA	Yes	No	No

Practise this dialogue with a partner, using the information in the table. A is British. Take turns to be A and B.

A: Can you advise me on visas and vaccinations?
B: Certainly. Where are you going?
A: Australia.
B: Well, you need a passport.
A: Will an Identity Card be sufficient?
B: No, I'm afraid not. A passport is required for travel to Australia.
A: And what about a visa?
B: A visa must be obtained before departure.
A: And vaccinations?
B: Vaccinations aren't necessary.
A: Thank you.
B: You're welcome.

Find similar information for your own and other countries and advise each other on requirements. Note that requirements for EEC citizens will be different than for non-EEC citizens within the European Community.

Exercise 4

Would you like to make some rules and regulations for your own classroom? The regulations can be serious or humorous. Write three such regulations, using the pattern 'must' + 'be' + past participle. Compare your regulations with those of other members of the class. An example of a humorous regulation would be:

Our teacher must be given a bouquet of roses on May 1st.

LESSON 48

He Said He'd Heard Something

Exercise 1

Choose True or False. Then write the sentences from the text that give the answers.

1 The marina manager forgot to speak to the security guard.
2 Meg thinks there is no danger.
3 Yolanda thinks the suspicious man is English.
4 The man told Yolanda he was a photographer.
5 Jack became suspicious while they were playing cards.
6 Jack saw someone in the water.
7 Jack wants to get home as quickly as possible.

Exercise 2

Reported Speech
Study the examples and complete the rule.

Man I've come to take photographs.
Yolanda *He said that he had come to take photographs.*

Jack I heard something.
Robert *He said he'd heard something.*

Rule: When the verb of reporting is in the Past Tense (eg 'said') then:

Direct speech verbs →	**Indirect speech**
Present Perfect	Past Perfect
eg I have come	eg ________.
Past Simple	Past Perfect
eg ________	eg ________

Sometimes we have to make other changes, eg 'yesterday' → 'the day before'; 'last week' → 'the week before'; 'my' → 'his/her', etc.

Change the following into reported speech.

Begin: *He/She said that* ________ and make any other changes necessary.

1 (The marina manager) 'I've already spoken to the security guard.'
2 (Robert) 'I've just received this radio message.'
3 (Man) 'I read about your expedition yesterday.'
4 (Meg) 'I've telephoned Geoff.'
5 (Yolanda) 'We found six packets of diamonds.'
6 (Yolanda) 'I enjoyed New York.'
7 (Robert) 'I didn't enjoy Lagos.'
8 (Jack) 'I didn't see anything strange.'

Exercise 3

Study the example and finish the rule.

Yolanda 'I have seen a suspicious character.'
Yolanda *said that* she had seen a suspicious character.
Yolanda *told me that* she had seen a suspicious character.
Yolanda *told Meg that* she had seen a suspicious character.

Rule: With indirect speech:
the verb 'say' is not followed by a noun or pronoun. (eg me, you, him, etc.)
the verb 'tell' is followed by a noun or ________.

(**Note:** with both 'say' and 'tell' we can omit 'that')

Study the dialogue. In pairs make up similar dialogues. Use the phrases to help you and be careful about 'he' and 'she'. Take turns to be A and B.

A: I met (1) John Carter yesterday.
B: Isn't he (2) a policeman?
A: No, I don't think so. He said that he had left (3) the police force.
B: That's funny. Last year, he told me (4) he had joined for life.
A: Well, he has changed his mind, then.
B: Yes, I suppose he has.

(1) Henry; Christopher; Rita; Jill Banks; Pauline Roberts

(2) a pilot; a bank manager; a teacher; a nurse; a university lecturer

(3) the school; the airline; the hospital; the bank; the university

(4) had signed a long term contract; had begun a special training course; had found a perfect job

Exercise 4

Interview someone in your class about their last holiday. Ask them:

Where did you go? How did you go there? Did you go with anybody? Where did you stay? What did you do? Did you enjoy the holiday?

Write a few sentences about the person's holiday, beginning each sentence with:

'*She/He told me that* . . . . .' or
'*She/He said that* . . . . .'

She's Got Funny, Little, Blue Eyes

Rob and Howard are in Lisbon, shopping for souvenirs.

Rob Here we are. This is the shop Marcos told me about.

Howard Ceramics, leather goods, jewellery. . . What a great place! It's got everything we need.

Rob You're right. You name it – they've got it. I'm going to buy all my presents here before we go back.

Howard What are you getting for Jane?

Rob Well, actually, I'm not sure. To tell you the truth, I hadn't really thought about it.

Howard Oh, come on, Rob! You must get her something. How about one of these beautiful, hand-painted, Portuguese vases?

Rob You're kidding. She hates vases. She gives them to her mother.

Howard Well, a scarf, then. What colour are her eyes?

Rob Blue . . . I think.

Howard Don't you know?

Rob Yes, they're blue. She's got funny, little, blue eyes.

Howard She sounds delightful. So, why don't you get her a little, blue, silk scarf to match her funny, little, blue eyes.

Rob A waste of money! She'd never wear it. She likes practical gifts.

Howard What an impossible woman! OK, Rob, I give up. Put an end to your problems and get her a large, round, heavy, iron cooking pot. You won't find anything more practical than that.

Rob Yes, and if our invisible saboteurs don't sink the yacht, that cooking pot certainly will. Forget about Jane. We've split up now anyway. Let's concentrate on you for a change. What are you getting?

Howard A bag.

Rob A leather bag?

Howard Of course. The Portuguese are famous for their leather goods.

Rob What colour do you want?

Howard Brown . . . a nice, brown bag.

Rob What kind of bag? Do you mean a briefcase?

Howard No, a handbag.

Rob I see. Are you buying something for Meg?

Howard How did you know?

Rob Well, I didn't think you were buying a smart, new, brown, Portuguese, leather handbag for yourself, Howard!

Howard Listen, you won't say anything about this to the others, will you, Rob?

Rob I won't . . . if you don't say anything to them about these.

Howard What are they? Handcuffs?

Rob Very funny. They're earrings.

Howard Very large, expensive, gold earrings by the look of them.

Rob Yes. The kind Yolanda likes. . .

Exercise 1

Read the dialogue and choose the best ending for each sentence.

1 Rob and Howard are shopping for souvenirs
   a) in a supermarket.
   b) in the capital of Portugal.
   c) in a furniture store.
2 Rob hadn't thought about
   a) telling the truth to Jane.
   b) the colour of Jane's eyes.
   c) getting Jane a present.
3 Jane wouldn't like a blue, silk scarf because
   a) she doesn't like blue.
   b) she would give it to her mother.
   c) she likes presents that are practical.
4 The iron cooking pot
   a) is a very practical gift.
   b) made the yacht sink.
   c) belongs to the saboteurs.

Exercise 2

Complete the chart with phrases from the dialogue. Note the order of items before the noun.

	Opinion	Size	Shape	Weight	Age	Colour & design	Country of origin	Material	Noun
	funny	little				blue			eyes
1									handbag
2									scarf
3									vases
4									earrings
5									cooking pot

Exercise 3

Make dialogues using the words below.

A: What are you getting for your (1) mother-in-law?
B: To tell you the truth, I hadn't really thought about it.
A: You must get him/her something. How about (2) some champagne?
B: You're kidding. He'd/She'd never (3) drink it/ them. He/She hates (4) champagne.
A: Why don't you get him/her (5) a silk scarf?
B: It's/They're a waste of money. He/She likes practical presents.
A: Well, get him/her (6) a cooking pot.
B: What a good idea!

(1) boss; girlfriend

(2) some earrings; some chocolates

(3) wear; eat

(4) earrings; chocolates

(5) a hand-painted vase; some cufflinks

(6) an interesting book; a calculator

Now invent dialogues about other people, for example: your best friend/your teacher/your dog.

Exercise 4

Rule: Study these examples.

What a coincidence! *What fascinating eyes!*
What a fantastic yacht! *What terrible coffee!*

Rewrite the sentences below in the form of exclamations.

1 This exam is easy. ____________
2 This place is great. ____________
3 That woman is impossible. ____________
4 These oranges are bitter. ____________
5 These paintings are colourful. ____________
6 This chocolate is horrible. ____________

Exercise 5

If you went on holiday, what presents would you bring back for the other students in your class, or for members of your family? Write about five people. Say what you would and wouldn't buy them and why. For example:

If I went to France, I would buy a present for Alessandra. I wouldn't buy her any perfume because she prefers to choose her own perfume. I'd buy her some French magazines because she's interested in fashion and she wants to improve her French.

LESSON 50

The Performance Lasts an Hour And a Half

Dorothy Walton is writing to her sister, Sylvia.

Dear Sylvia,

It was lovely to see you last Sunday. I was going to telephone you when I got back, but there's no need to spend money on calls, is there? It's so much cheaper and easier to send a letter. I'm sure you agree.

Geoffrey arrived home on Wednesday. I collected him at the airport. He was in a pitiful state. He hobbled off the aeroplane with one leg in plaster. He said it wasn't serious and the plaster was only a precaution. You can imagine how I felt! The journey from Sydney lasted 26 hours and poor Geoffrey was exhausted when he arrived. His luggage weighed over 35 kilos and the excess weight cost us £60. It was mostly alcohol too! Of course, I blame Jack Craig for all this. What a terrible troublemaker! I've told Geoffrey over and over again, but he takes no notice. Perhaps he'll take my word for it now.

About the show on Tuesday: you said that there were no more tickets. You were right, but guess what? I've managed to get two. Simon (the young motorcycle messenger from Grosvenor Express) knows the assistant director of the theatre and he managed to book the seats for us. Normally one ticket costs £9. Guess how much I paid? The two tickets cost £12. Isn't that a wonderful saving? Simon's such a sweet, considerate boy. You know, he even came to help in the office when Suzy was away with the 'flu. You'll probably meet Simon when you come to London on Tuesday because he's offered to drive me to the station. I've checked the timetable and your train gets in at 6.45. I'll meet you at Victoria and then Simon will take us both to the theatre. The doors open at 7.30 and the performance lasts an hour and a half. We don't have to worry about getting home either. Simon is going to wait at the Institute and will pick us up when the show ends. Aren't we lucky?

I look forward to seeing you soon.

All my love,

Dorothy

Exercise 1

Read Dorothy's letter. Here are the answers to some questions. Write the questions.

1 When ______________________________?
Last Sunday.
2 When ______________________________?
On Wednesday.
3 What ______________________________?
It was in plaster.
4 Where ______________________________?
To a show.
5 Who ______________________________?
Simon did. He knows the assistant director of the theatre.
6 What ______________________________?
He came in to help in the office.

Exercise 2

The words and phrases in A are in the letter. Underline them as you read. Then match them with the definitions in B.

A

1 there's no need
2 in a pitiful state
3 hobbled
4 excess
5 troublemaker
6 takes no notice
7 take my word for it
8 away
9 gets in

B

a) walked with difficulty
b) not at work
c) believe me
d) arrives
e) doesn't listen
f) it's not necessary
g) a person who causes trouble
h) extra
i) looked terrible

Rule:
The jacket costs £97. He weighs 70 kilos.
The journey lasted a long time.

'Last', 'weigh' and ________ are verbs of measurement. They are usually followed by a unit of measurement.

Find more examples of them in Dorothy's letter and complete the sentences.

1 ______________________________ 26 hours.
2 ______________________________ £12.
3 ______________________________ over 35 kilos.
4 ______________________________ an hour and a half.
5 ______________________________ £60.

Exercise 3

Complete the dialogue with the words and phrases below and then practise it with your partner.

lovely to see you	how much I paid
two hours	the performance
saving	I paid £9
getting home	cost £11
my sister came to pick me up	to see a play last Friday night

A: It's *lovely to see you*. Have you been anywhere interesting lately?
B: Yes, I went ________.
A: How long did ________ last?
B: It lasted ________.
A: Was it expensive?
B: Guess ________?
A: I don't know.
B: The tickets normally ________, but ________.
A: What a wonderful ________! Aren't you lucky?
B: Yes, and I didn't have to worry about ________ because ________________.

Try to invent other dialogues like this one.

Exercise 4

Make notes about something special that your partner has done recently or in the past. It can be a visit to a place he/she has visited or a film, play or show he/ she has seen. Try to remember all the details, like this:

What:	*a journey*
Date:	*23 April*
From:	*London*
To:	*Liverpool*
Journey time:	*2½ hours*
Cost:	*£45 one way, £65 return*
Time of departure:	9.30
Time of arrival:	12.00

Write a short report from your notes. Begin like this:

On the 23 April, Pietro went on a journey from . . . . .

I Had to Work Hard to Get That Degree

Meg Ah, so here you are! Why are you here all by yourself?

Howard Well, sometimes it gets a bit noisy below deck with the others.

Meg I know exactly what you mean. So you came on deck to get some peace and quiet.

Howard Yes, and simply to enjoy the evening and watch the stars. It's such a wonderful night! It reminds me of nights I've spent in the forest. So tranquil . . .

Meg You surprise me, Howard. You know, I suspect you must be quite a romantic at heart.

Howard Maybe I am. Who knows? I do know that basically I'm a quiet person.

Meg But you always have plenty to say. That's what seems to cause most of the arguments.

Howard So you've noticed.

Meg Sorry, Howard, I didn't mean to seem rude.

Howard You're right, of course. I upset people. Maybe I do it to attract attention. Every man needs a little attention to boost his ego.

Meg What! Even a self-confident chap like you?

Howard Do I seem very sure of myself?

Meg You give everyone that impression. We feel quite intimidated by you sometimes.

Howard That was the problem I had at school and university. You see, I'm not especially gifted. I had to work hard to get my degree in forestry and I was hopeless at school subjects. I used to study until the early hours of the morning to finish my homework. I always got good results and the other kids thought I was a genius. In fact I couldn't do anything.

Meg I can't believe that, Howard. What about sailing? You do that well. You're a natural.

Howard That's what you think. I was pretty hopeless at sailing too. I used to give up my weekends to work on other people's boats. I wanted to be the best in order to impress the other kids. I was a perfectionist. It's ironical. I tried hard to win their admiration and it just made me more unpopular.

Meg But that's in the past. Things have changed. You're different now.

Exercise 1

Read the dialogue and answer these questions.

1 Where are Meg and Howard?
2 Why did Howard go on deck?
3 What type of person is Howard?
4 What causes most of the arguments on the *Ocean Explorer?*
5 What does Howard do to attract attention?
6 What did Howard study at university?
7 Why did Howard always get good results at school?
8 Is Howard a 'natural' sailor?
9 Why did Howard want to be the best?
10 Did Howard win the admiration of the other kids?

Exercise 2

Find words or phrases in the dialogue that mean the same as these words and phrases.

1 alone ________
2 a lot ________
3 very impolite ________
4 make people angry ________
5 make him feel important ________
6 man ________
7 talented ________
8 not very good ________

How do these sentences end? Read the dialogue again to find out.

9 I do it ________.
10 I used to give up my weekends ________.
11 Every man needs a little attention ________.
12 I had to work hard ________.
13 I wanted to be the best ________.
14 I used to study all night ________.

Rule: The second part of each sentence answers the question 'why'? We begin the second part of each sentence with 'to' or ________ ________ ________ + the verb.

Exercise 3

Complete the dialogue with the phrases below, and practise it with a partner.

a) Why are you going there?
b) What for?
c) Why should I buy one of those?
d) Why are you phoning?
e) Your English is fine. Why do you need to improve it?

A: ________
B: To cancel our appointment. I'm flying to England tomorrow.
A: ________
B: To improve my English, of course.
A: ________
B: In order to get good results in the exam.
A: You surprise me! You should save your money.
B: ________
A: To buy a video cassette recorder.
A: ________
B: In order to watch English language films.

Exercise 4

Work with your partner. Write a list of the names of ten everyday objects. When you have finished, give your list to another pair of students.

Select five out of the ten objects on your new list. Now imagine this situation. Your car has broken down in the middle of the jungle. There is no special equipment in your car, but in the boot you find five objects in your new list. Explain how you would use the objects to escape from the jungle.

Write sentences like this:

I would use the X________ to Y________.

LESSON 52

Taking Photos Is So Difficult

Exercise 1

Choose True or False. Then write the sentences from the text that give the answers.

1 Jack doesn't feel frightened at sea.
2 Yolanda thinks Jack spends too much money in bars.
3 Yolanda thinks that the Nevada is impressive.
4 The inflatable follows the dolphins.
5 After the explosion Meg doesn't know where Howard is.
6 Howard finds a second mine.
7 Jack is worried about Howard.

Exercise 2

Sailing gives me a thrill.
We can use the '-ing' form of the verb as the subject.

Photographing dolphins is difficult.
We can use the '-ing' form of the verb plus noun as subject.

Complete the sentences by choosing words from the list below, and putting the verb into the '-ing' form.

jump out of the sea – radio for help – cut through the water – take good photographs – inspect the hull of the boat – spend his money in bars

1 _________ gives Jack a thrill.
2 _________ gives Yolanda a thrill.
3 _________ took Howard about ten minutes.
4 _________ was one of Jack's bad habits.
5 _________ was easy, as the explosion hadn't damaged the equipment.
6 _________ seems to be a favourite pastime of dolphins.

Exercise 3

Yolanda If you like spaces, you should visit the desert.

Now study the dialogue, and make up similar dialogues. Take turns to be A and B.

A: I'm trying to learn (1) French.
B: Well, if you want to learn French, you should go to (2) Paris.
A: I've been there. I think I'll go to (2) Lyons.
B: That's a good idea. Living in (3) France is the best way to learn French.

(1) German; Portuguese; Greek; Italian; Arabic; Japanese; Spanish

(2) Madrid; Osaka; Stuttgart; Lisbon; Rome; Cairo; Tokyo; Athens; Barcelona; Salonica; Oporto; Lyons; Berlin Turin; Alexandria

(3) Italy; Germany; Spain; Japan; an Arab country; Portugal; Greece

Exercise 4

Write about yourself. What is your favourite pastime? What are your bad habits? What gives you a thrill? You may use sentences similar to those in Exercise 2.

LESSON 53

I Should Contact Them If I Were You

The Portuguese Police have contacted their British colleagues. Eduardo Soares is talking on the phone to Eric Stubbs.

Eduardo Hello Eric. This is Eduardo from the Portuguese Police – you remember we met on the European Police Course in Reading last year?

Eric Eduardo, nice to hear from you. How is everything?

Eduardo Fine, and you? Wife and kids OK?

Eric Fine, thanks. But you're not calling for that! What can I do for you?

Eduardo It's like this, Eric. Have you heard about the *Ocean Explorer*?

Eric Yeah! Going round the world to raise money. Diamonds were found aboard in New York, right?

Eduardo Right. And a couple of hours ago there was an explosion on board – while they were crossing the Bay of Biscay. The boat's still floating, and nobody was hurt. A French naval boat will arrive there tomorrow.

Eric I see. And you don't think it was an accident?

Eduardo I think that smugglers are involved somewhere. A group of suspicious characters crossed into Portugal from Badajoz recently.

Eric Well, maybe they had something to do with the *Ocean Explorer*. We searched the owner's house and boatyard in England, but found nothing. Now what about the French? Have you contacted them?

Eduardo Not yet.

Eric I should contact them if I were you. Ask for Bistes, Paris Agency – tell him you're a friend of mine. He'd help you, if you asked him. Mention my name. We had a great time at a seminar in Tenerife last year!

Eduardo Thanks! Now, I'd like another favour, if you could.

Eric Sure.

Eduardo An Englishman called James Winstanley arrived in Lisbon just before the *Ocean Explorer* left. He was seen with the Badajoz gang, and also at the marina. We haven't questioned him yet. His hotel record says he's aged 35, lives at 22 Holland Avenue, Manchester, and is a teacher. But he doesn't look like a teacher to me. Could you check that as soon as possible?

Eric Leave it with me Eduardo. . . . .

At 11.30 this fax is handed to Eduardo.

Anthony Wilkins alias James Robert Winstanley. Fair hair, blue eyes. Height 6 feet 2 inches. Current address 11a Grand Drive, Southampton. Ex-naval Special Boat Squadron. Received dishonourable discharge from the Navy for safe blowing while on leave. Two convictions, both for safe blowing. An explosives expert. Works occasionally as a diving instructor.

Good luck,

Eric

Exercise 1

Choose True or False. Then write the sentences from the text that give the answers.

1 Eduardo Soares knows Eric Stubbs.
2 Eric Stubbs isn't married.
3 The boat sank after the explosion.
4 Eric tells Eduardo to contact the French Police.
5 Eduardo wants to check on James Winstanley.
6 Anthony Wilkins (alias James Winstanley) knows about explosives and diving.

Complete this police form for Wilkins.

Family name:	Wilkins
First name(s):	
Height:	
Hair:	
Colour of eyes:	
Address:	

Exercise 2

More sentences with 'If':

He would help you, if you asked him.
(He'd help you, if you asked him.)

Are you going to ask him? Perhaps.
Remember with this type of conditional sentence.

Main clause: 'would' + verb	**'If' clause:** Verb in Past Simple (eg 'asked')

Now join the two halves of each sentence.

A

1 The police would arrest all the smugglers
2 Eric would contact the French Police
3 Bistes would help Eduardo
4 Anthony Wilkins would be arrested
5 Yolanda would buy some new photographic equipment
6 Robert would go back to the oil business

B

a) if he wanted to make a lot of money.
b) if Eduardo asked him.
c) if he was Eduardo.
d) if she had more money.
e) if the Portuguese Police caught him.
f) if they knew them.

Exercise 3

Study the dialogue. Make similar dialogues using the phrases to help you.

A: I'd like to learn about (1) boats.
B: (2) John would tell you a lot about boats if you asked him.
A: But he doesn't look like a (3) sailor to me.
B: Well, he isn't a sailor. But he knows about boats.

(1) racing cars; computers; the European Economic Community; Egypt; flying; mountain climbing; France

(2) Mary; Massoud; Pierre; Françoise

(3) Frenchman/woman; racing driver; mountaineer; pilot; economist; Egyptian; computer programmer

Exercise 4

If you had one week of complete freedom, how would you spend it?
Say what you would do, where you would go, how you would spend your money, etc. You may begin like this:

If I had a week of complete freedom, I would . . . . .

LESSON 54

I Don't Know What to Do about Him

The *Ocean Explorer* is waiting for help. Meg is re-reading a letter from her mother.

Dear Meg,

I hope you're keeping well. It seems a long time since I heard from you, but I suppose there aren't many letter boxes in the middle of the Ocean! Everyone here is quite well. Mrs Armstrong sends her love.

I've still got a pain in my arm. I've been to the physiotherapist, and she told me what to do. I have to swing my arm backwards and forwards for one minute every day. It hurts a bit, but she makes me do it regularly, and it's getting better.

Your father has got a nasty cold. He's been taking some medicine for it, but it isn't doing much good. I don't know what to do about him. I can't make him go to the doctor. You know how he hates it.

I did some babysitting for Carole Royce last Saturday. They have two little boys, Dan (7) and Tim (8). I didn't know how to switch their TV on, but Dan showed me what to do. I do love little children.

Do you remember Ann Hornby? She was in the same class as you at Oldlands. She got married last week to Alan somebody – a psychologist. It was such a nice wedding. Ann says she'd like four children, two boys and two girls. I think four is too many these days – the thought makes me feel quite exhausted!

The weather is getting warmer these days – spring is definitely in the air. Do take care, Meg. Write as soon as you can.

Love, Mummy

PS: That nice Ian Clarke was asking about you. He's now the consultant surgeon at Mandley Hospital – not married yet.

Meg Poor mummy! She can't wait to be a grandmother!

Exercise 1

Answer the following questions.

1 Has Meg read this letter before? How do you know?
2 Has Meg's mother received a letter from her recently?
3 Who do you think Mrs Armstrong is?
4 What did the physiotherapist tell Meg's mother to do?
5 Who did Meg's mother do some babysitting for?
6 What is Oldlands? How do you know?
7 What does Meg's mother want Meg to do? (Write one or two things.)

Exercise 2

Study the examples. Then complete the sentences, using the phrases below.

The physiotherapist told me *what to do.*
Dan showed me *how to do everything.*

how to switch on the TV; what to order; how to sail the *Ocean Explorer*; how to cook Dutch food; how to operate the radar system; where to go

1 Meg's mother didn't know ________ in the Royce's house.
2 Rob was lost. He didn't know ________. Luckily he met Yolanda, and she showed him the way.
3 In a Brazilian restaurant Rob didn't know ________. Fortunately Yolanda was with him.
4 At first, Howard didn't know ________, but very soon Jack showed him.
5 Lisa showed Jack ________.
6 Rob showed Meg ________.

Exercise 3

'The physiotherapist *makes me swing my arm.*' Study the dialogue, then make up similar dialogues. Take turns to be A and B.

A: Why are you (1) swinging your arm?
B: The (2) doctor makes me do it.
A: Well the doctor wouldn't make me do it!
B: But you haven't got (3) a pain in your arm.

(1) rubbing your leg; reading your grammar book; practising your violin; adding up your expenses; repeating the English irregular verbs; practising your saxaphone; collecting receipts for everything

(2) music teacher; English teacher; accountant

(3) a pain in your leg/foot; a tax problem; an English test tomorrow; a music examination

Exercise 4

Write a list of things that people make you do. Say who it is, and what they make you do, eg

X makes me . . . . .

If you cannot think of anything, think of the time when you were a little child. Make sentences with 'used to', eg

X used to make me . . . . .

LESSON 55

They Seem to Be Stopping in Every Port

Geoffrey and his wife Dorothy are looking at their garden.

Dorothy Well, dear, the spring flowers seem to be coming late this year. It's already April and they're only just starting.

Geoffrey Well, everything's late this year.

Dorothy And another thing that's late is the *Ocean Explorer*. What's happening to them? They seem to be stopping in every port, and they seem to be having the most extraordinary accidents. I imagine it's that Jack! He can never pass an open bar, nor resist a pretty girl. And at his age! He seems to create all the problems!

Geoffrey I don't know. He doesn't seem to create absolutely every problem. In fact, he often seems to be very useful for the expedition. He's not so bad.

Dorothy Not so bad! I remember Jack telephoning at midnight once, and I also remember you going out with him!

Geoffrey Be fair Dorothy – that was an exception – Jack and I hadn't seen old Henry for ten years – and he only had a couple of hours in Heathrow before going back to Nebraska!

Dorothy Well anyway, I hope you've learned your lesson from this last episode – going to parties in Sydney in the small hours, and ending up in hospital! But how is your foot today?

Geoffrey Much better. In fact, it seems to be recovering very quickly. A good thing too, because I'll have a lot of meetings and interviews when the *Ocean Explorer* returns!

Dorothy If it ever does – I don't think it'll ever get back. How's the rescue fund, by the way?

Geoffrey About £20 000 to go.

Dorothy Surely the University won't worry about £20 000 when you've raised £480 000.

Geoffrey I'm not so sure, Dorothy. The Vice-Chancellor – Leafe – is a hard man. If we fail, the Institute will close! Oh, there's the phone.

Dorothy I'll go.

One minute later . . .

Dorothy You'd better come to the phone dear . . . it's the British Consulate in Toulon. Your boat seems to be sinking in the Bay of Biscay!!

Exercise 1

Choose True or False. Then write the sentences from the text that give you the answers.

1 The spring flowers in Dorothy's garden usually start in April.
2 Geoffrey thinks the plants are slow this year.
3 Dorothy thinks the *Ocean Explorer* is coming home quickly.
4 Dorothy thinks Jack has caused the problems.
5 Geoffrey didn't know Henry.
6 Geoffrey's foot is getting better.
7 If the fund reaches £480 000 the Institute will continue.
8 The *Ocean Explorer* has arrived in Toulon.

Exercise 2

Study these examples:

He *creates* all the problems.
He *seems to create* all the problems.
He *doesn't seem to* create all the problems.

They *are stopping* in every port.
They *seem to be stopping* in every port.
They *don't seem to be stopping* in every port.

Change the following sentences in the same way by using 'seem'.

1 The flowers are coming late this year.
2 Yolanda takes a lot of photographs.
3 The *Ocean Explorer* is having the most extraordinary accidents.
4 Howard doesn't like bad weather.
5 Jack is very useful for the expedition.
6 Lisa likes dolphins.
7 The flowers aren't coming quickly this year.
8 Geoff's foot is recovering very quickly.
9 The *Ocean Explorer* is sinking in the Bay of Biscay.
10 Geoff works very hard at the Institute.

Exercise 3

'*I remember Jack telephoning* us at midnight once.'
Study the six pictures and words, then work in pairs.
(A) closes his/her book and describes all the pictures. Begin each sentence with '*I remember* .....'
(B) has the book open and checks what (A) says. Then (B) closes the book and describes the pictures, while (A) checks.

Example:

A: *I remember John drinking a glass of wine.*
B: *That's right.* (*or No, that's wrong.*)

1 John – drink 2 Maria – read
3 Carmen – take 4 Antonio – write
5 Jean-Pierre – drive 6 Anna – eat

Exercise 4

Try to remember a recent situation where you were with some other people. Describe the scene. Say who was there, then what you remember them doing, eg

I was in a café with X, Y and Z. I remember X ordering a coffee .....

LESSON 56

They Were Going to Cherbourg When I Called Them

Exercise 1

Choose True or False. Then write the sentences from the text that give the answers.

1 *La Bretagne* was leaving Cherbourg when Rob contacted her.
2 Howard thinks that he can see a ship.
3 The *Ocean Explorer* might sink at any moment.
4 Yolanda asks the French officer to stay still.
5 It will be difficult to repair the damage.
6 The team receive a cheque from the Mayor of Cherbourg.

Exercise 2

Study the examples.

You were sleeping when we called you.

The Past Continuous is sometimes used to contrast a continuous action in the past with a short action that occurs during the continuous action.

They were going to Cherbourg.

The Past Continuous is also used when the action in the past is not finished, or when the speaker (writer) is not concerned about the end of the action.

Study the dialogue. In pairs, make up similar dialogues. Use the phrases to help you.

A: (1) Jack was very busy (2) last night.
B: Was he?
A: Yes. He was (3) repairing the hole in the boat.
B: Well I'm glad I wasn't repairing the hole in the boat.
A: So am I.

(1) Yolanda; Meg; Rob; Lisa; Howard

(2) last week; yesterday; last year; a few years ago; an hour ago

(3) buying a lot of souvenirs; working on a marine project; cooking an enormous meal; writing a lot of letters

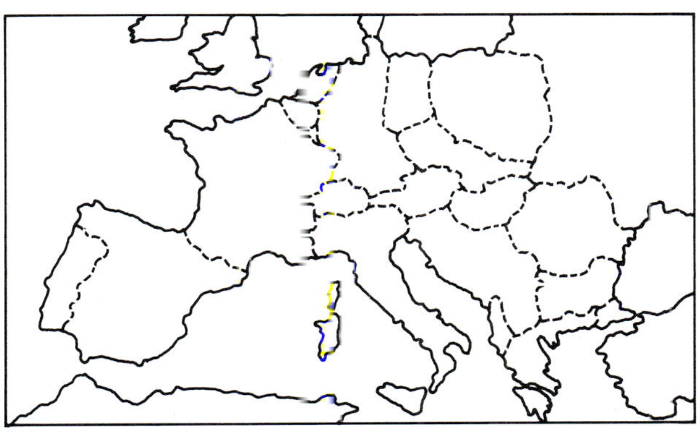

Exercise 3

The expression 'to look like'

Look at the people, and make sentences like the following:

The man with the cigar looks like the man with the dog.

Exercise 4

Find a map of the Mediterranean or of the world. Look at the shapes of the different countries. Write sentences about five countries using 'look like', eg

X looks like a dog's leg.

LESSON 57

It Took More Time Than We Had Anticipated

Antonia Harte, of Atlantic TV, is interviewing Meg about the expedition for her next *World Wide* programme.

Antonia So, you've got only two days to go before the end of the rescue fund appeal.

Meg Yes, that's right. It seems years since we began.

Antonia About six months ago, I think.

Meg Seven and a half, actually. We thought it would take six months to complete the voyage, but it took six weeks more than we had anticipated because there were lots of problems along the way.

Antonia Ah, yes. There was that trouble in America.

Meg Yes, first there was the storm. It lasted hours. Then the diamonds were discovered.

Antonia How many did you find?

Meg Well, the customs told us that they had a street value of about 20 million dollars.

Antonia A fortune!

Meg It certainly was. And one fortieth of it would have solved the Institute's problems. Anyway, after New York, we sailed to the Caribbean and from there we went to Recife.

Antonia Ah, Recife. It's a fascinating place. The West African tradition is very strong in that part of Brazil, especially in religion – you know, Macumba, Condomble.

Meg Well, there was certainly some black magic in Recife. Someone set fire to the boat. No one was hurt, fortunately. Anyway, after that we sailed down the east coast of Latin America and round Cape Horn. Luckily, the next stage, across the Pacific took less than we had planned, in spite of the business in Tobanau.

Antonia So, you really were Down Under.

Meg Yes, and the appeal fund is still down, too.

Antonia Well, let's hope that tomorrow's *World Wide* programme puts it right on top.

Exercise 1

Answer the following questions.

1 The expedition took
   a) several years.
   b) seven and a half months.
   c) about six months.
2 What is interesting about Recife?
3 What would one fortieth of $20 million be?
4 Why was that amount so important?
5 Why does Meg say that there was 'some black magic in Recife'?
6 How will Antonia's programme help the appeal fund?

Exercise 2

The round-the-world voyage took more time than anticipated. Complete the table and the sentence below.

A: Planned or anticipated time	B: Actual time	C: Difference between A and B
six months	seven and a half months	

The journey took ________ *longer than anticipated.*
(or *'than they had anticipated'*)
The table below gives more variations on this pattern.

It took	half an hour one hour two hours etc. one day one week one month	two days, etc. two weeks, etc. two months, etc.	longer more less	than	we had anticipated.

Write four sentences of your own, using the above pattern, and following the example given below.

Example:

Meg and the crew thought it would take six months to sail round the world, but in fact it took six weeks more than they had anticipated because there were many problems along the way.

Exercise 3

A and B arranged to meet. B has just arrived. Practise this dialogue with a partner. Take turns to be A and B.

A: Hello. You're (1) late.
B: Yes. (2) Driving via the M25 took a lot longer than I had anticipated.
A: Really? (3) How annoying.
B: Yes, I thought it would take (4) an hour at the most.
A: How long did it take?
B: (5) Nearly two hours.
A: (5) Nearly two hours!
You'll need to allow (6) more time in future.

(1) early

(2) Coming by train took less time than I'd anticipated.*

(3) How fortunate.

(4) two hours at least*

(5) Just an hour.*

(6) less time in future

* Use information and times of your own.

Exercise 4

Solve the following puzzles and make up two of your own. Exchange with a partner and answer your partner's questions.

We planned to spend $65.00 a day. It cost us $15.00 per day less than we had planned, so we stayed for four days instead of three. How much did it cost us altogether?

I planned to reach home by 4 o'clock, but my car wouldn't start, so the journey took me an hour and a half longer than I had planned. What time did I finally reach home?

LESSON 58

I Don't Know Who to Ask

Lisa wants to give Jack a surprise on his birthday.
But discovering where he lives is a problem.

OCEAN INSTITUTE
MESSAGE

Howard

You weren't here when I called. I don't know who to ask, so I hope you can help. I want to know where Jack lives. It's his birthday next week, and I want to give him a surprise. Don't tell him! Lisa

I don't know where he lives. Why don't you ask Meg? Howard

No, I don't know what his address is and I don't know who to ask. It should be on his file, so why don't you ask Suzy? Meg

Suzy, can you check? Lisa

I've checked. His old address is on file. He left there before you went on the expedition. I'll ask him where he lives now and then I'll let you know. Suzy.

Memo

From: Suzy Foster

To: Jack Craig

Change of Address

I think you have a new address now. Could you complete this form for the records? Thanks.

Name: ______________________

Address: ______________________

____

Telephone Number: ______________________

Exercise 1

Answer the following questions.

1 What does Lisa want to find out?
2 Why does she want to know?
3 Who does Lisa ask first?
4 Who does she ask next?
5 Does this person have the information Lisa wants?
6 How will Suzy find out the information Lisa wants?

Exercise 2

In her note, Lisa uses this sentence:

I don't know who to ask.

The same pattern can be used with other 'wh-' words and 'how', as shown in the table.

I	don't know	who	to ask. to see.
He She	doesn't know	where	to go.
We	don't know	when	to leave.
		what	to do.
		how	to do it.

Write appropriate sentences based on the examples in the table for the following situations.

Example:

A friend is arriving later today by plane. (meet)
I don't know when to meet him.

1 Lisa has bought a new tin opener. The instructions are missing. (use)
2 The film has jammed in Howard's camera. (remove)
3 Jack's car has broken down. (fix)
4 My computer has lost some data. (retrieve)
5 Rob wants to post some letters in the Canaries. (post)
6 Yolanda wants some information on processing her films. (ask)
7 Meg wants to send a fax to Geoffrey. (arrange)
8 Geoffrey wants to get his wife a birthday present. (buy)
9 We want to have a really nice meal tonight. (go)
10 You're flying from an unfamiliar airport. (check in)

Exercise 3

Practise the dialogue with a partner. B is a stranger and needs help. Take turns to be A and B.

A: Can I help you?
B: Yes. I don't know (1) where to go.
A: (2) Who are you looking for?
B: I'm looking for (3) someone who can cash a Eurocheque.
A: Ah, in that case you should (3) go to the foreign exchange department. It's next to the cashier.
B: Thank you.
A: Glad I could help.

(1) what to do; who to see; who to ask*

(2) What are you looking for? Where are you going? What do you want to know?*

(3) something to cure my headache; somewhere to get a cup of coffee; someone to repair my camera*

(4) go to a pharmacist. There's one nearby.; go to the coffee shop. It's on the ground floor.; go to the camera shop. It's just round the corner.*

* Use information of your own.

Exercise 4

You have been asked to write some advertising information to help visitors to your town. First, make a list of some of the things visitors usually want to know. Second, write the advice, following the examples.

Do you have problems? You don't know where to dine out?
If you want somewhere to have a good Italian meal, go to La Gioconda.
And you don't know what to take home as a souvenir?
If you're looking for something special to take home, go to Sterne's the Jewellers.

LESSON 59

She's the Best Person to Ask for Advice

London, Soho

Robert wants to return Yolanda's hospitality in New York, but he isn't sure where to take her in London.

Robert Howard, can you give me some advice?
Howard Sure, Rob. How can I help?
Robert Well, I want to take Yolanda out this weekend, but I'm not sure where to go.
Howard I don't believe it! I thought you were a real man of the world now.
Robert Yes, well, what do you suggest for dinner on Saturday night? I thought of going to Mac's Diner in Soho.
Howard Mac's Diner! That's the last place to go for a good meal.
Robert Maybe, but the music's great. And they serve really good American style food.
Howard Depends, really. It's not the first place to choose for good jazz. I think Dizzie Murphy's is the best.
Robert Right. But what about dinner? I hear Gourmet Gourmand is very good.
Howard It's very trendy and a meal there costs an arm and a leg. Anyway, I'm really not the best person to ask for advice on food and wine. Meg is. And here she is.
Meg Hi, Rob. You look worried.
Robert Oh, no. I'm not worried. I need some advice.
Meg Oh, really. What do you want to know?
Robert Meg. What's the best place to take Yolanda for a good meal? Not too expensive, but good.
Meg Well, I'd recommend the Bay Tree in Soho. It's good, but not too expensive. I'm sure Yolanda would like it.
Robert Thanks, Meg. Howard said you were the best person to ask for advice on dining out.
Meg He did! He hasn't taken my advice himself. Not for some time.
Howard Ah, Meg. How about going out to dinner on Saturday?
Meg Why, Howard, how can I resist such an invitation? How about Gourmet Gourmand?
Howard What?!
Robert Well, Howard, you did say she was the best person to ask!

Exercise 1

Complete the following sentences.

1 The last place for a good meal is ________.
2 ________ is Dazzie Murphy's in Soho.
3 The most expensive place for ________ is ________.
4 ________ for a good meal is ________.
5 The best person ________ for advice is ________.

Now answer these questions.

6 Where will Yolanda and Rob have dinner?
7 Where will Megan and Howard have dinner?
8 Who has an unwelcome surprise?

Exercise 2

There are variations on this sentence in the dialogue.

She's the best person to ask for advice on dining out.

The pattern is:
'X is the best/first/worst/last/etc. person/place/etc. to' + verb

Find all the examples of this pattern in the dialogue.

Match the two parts to make complete sentences.

1 Holland is the best place to go . . . . .
2 Venice is the best place to visit . . . . .
3 An Indian restaurant is the best place to go . . . . .
4 Italy is the best place to go . . . . .
5 Egypt is the last place to go . . . . .
6 Gourmet Gourmand is the last place to go . . . . .

a) . . . . . for delicious ice cream.
b) . . . . . for cheap, tasty food.
c) . . . . . for hot, spicy food.
d) . . . . . for a climbing holiday.
e) . . . . . for a skiing vacation.
f) . . . . . for canals and beautiful glassware.

Now write three similar sentences of your own.

Exercise 3

A asks B for advice. Practise the dialogue. Take turns to be A and B.

A: Can you give me some advice?
B: Sure. How can I help?
A: Well, I want (1) to dine out on Saturday night.
B: (2) Gourmet Gourmand is the best place to go for French cooking.
A: Oh, I was really looking for (3) Italian style food.
B: Well, in that case, (4) La Gioconda is the best place to go.
A: Thanks. That's very helpful.
B: Glad I could advise you.

(1) go to a show; buy a new jacket*

(2) La Trocadero is the best place to go to for an evening out.; Giorgio's is the best shop to go for a smart jacket.*

(3) a play; something less trendy*

(4) The Albany Theatre; The Top Shop*

* Use your own information.

Exercise 4

Write an entry for a good food and entertainment guide for your town or a town near you. The article is to go in a magazine for tourists. Use the patterns you have practised in this and the previous lesson.

LESSON 60

I'm Going to Take a Look

Exercise 1

Choose True or False. Then write the sentences from the text that give the answers.

1 Jack doesn't suspect Otto.
2 Otto seems to spend more money than he makes.
3 Jack decides to go to the boatyard.
4 Jack's key doesn't work.
5 Yolanda decides to help Jack.
6 Bergman's friend has plenty of time.
7 Jack is going to keep quiet about Bergman.

Exercise 2

Study the example.

Jack *I'll take a chance.*

The verb 'take' can be used with many different nouns, eg *take a holiday*.
(Often it means the same as 'have' in these cases.)

Complete the sentences, and use the correct form of 'take' + noun (you may use the same noun more than once).

take a drink; a look; a glance; a break; a holiday; a rest; a chance

1 Jack decided ________ at Bergman's boatyard.
2 Everything was quiet at the yard, so Jack ________ and went in.
3 When he has his next holiday, Rob ________ in Scotland.
4 Howard ________ because he felt thirsty.
5 You've been writing that report all day. Why ________ (you-not) ________?
6 As Yolanda walked quickly along the street, she ________ at her watch.
7 ________ (you) ________ yet this year? Yes, I went to Portugal.

Exercise 3

Study the dialogue. In pairs, make up similar dialogues. Take turns to be A and B.

A: You seem (1) to be working very hard these days.
B: Yes, I'm going (2) to take an exam next week.
A: Oh, you're going to take an exam! Do you feel (3) nervous about it?
B: No, I don't feel nervous. I feel quite (4) confident.
A: I'm glad to hear it.

(1) to be preparing a lot of food this morning; to be going to France a lot these days; to be writing a lot this year; to be jogging a lot these days; to be saving a lot of money this year; to be decorating your rooms a lot these days

(2) to run the London marathon next month; to organize a conference in Paris next month; to sell the house next month; to publish a novel next year; to give a big dinner party tonight; to go on an expensive African safari next month

(3) worried; tense

(4) happy; relaxed

Exercise 4

What sort of things do tourists smuggle into your country and out of your country? How do they usually try to do it?

What Else Has Changed?

Jack, Lisa and Rob are back at the International Ocean Institute in London.

Suzy Hi, Jack. Welcome back, Lisa.
Jack Well, it's great to be back. The old place looks just the same.
Lisa How do you know? You've never worked here.
Jack Maybe not, but I have been here a few times.
Lisa Well, not as often as me, and I'm telling you that it's changed. Suzy, you've moved your desk for a start and you aren't using a typewriter any more. I see you're using a word processor now.
Rob And you've changed your hairstyle.
Suzy Do you like it?
Rob Not bad, not bad.
Jack What's that on the wall behind your desk?
Suzy It's a poster of Chicken 'n Chips.
Jack Pardon?
Suzy Chicken 'n Chips. Haven't you heard of them? They've been Number One in the charts for the past three weeks.
Lisa You're a bit out of touch, Jack. It's the name of a group. Everyone knows that. It's a boy and two girls.
Suzy Well, not exactly. One of the girls has left and another boy has joined the group in her place. Now it's two boys and one girl.
Jack Well, Lisa?
Lisa OK. I'm out of touch, too. I feel as though I've been away for a million years. Even the street has changed. Who's that shifty-looking character I saw outside? I haven't seen him before.
Suzy The chap with the bike, the black leather jacket and the big boots?
Lisa That's the one.
Suzy That's Simon, our friendly motorcycle messenger.
Jack He doesn't look very friendly to me. In fact I don't like the look of him at all.
Suzy Neither do I, but he does his job well and Mrs Walton likes him.
Rob What else has changed?
Suzy Have you looked across the street?
Lisa Goodness! What's going on over there?
Suzy They're pulling down the old houses and they're building a new, luxury hotel.
Lisa But we don't want any hotels in this area. Hotels attract tourists, and tourists make prices rise. That's the last thing we want.
Jack Yes, I think it's awful. What's Geoff doing about it? He'd better make a complaint right away.
Rob Why are you getting so hot under the collar, Jack? Those houses are an eyesore.
Jack It's very simple, Rob. If they build a hotel there, it will block our access to the pub. And that's serious.

Exercise 1

There have been some changes in and around the International Ocean Institute. Find sentences in the dialogue about changes to the following people and things.

1 Suzy's desk

2 the old houses

3 the street

4 Suzy's typewriter

5 the girls in Chicken 'n Chips

6 Suzy's hairstyle

7 the hotel

8 the boy in Chicken 'n Chips

Exercise 2

Here is part of a report from Geoffrey to the University of Wessex. Fill in the spaces with verbs in the Present Simple, the Present Continuous or the Present Perfect. Choose from these verbs:

contact use gain develop offer have
wait sell appear earn apply give
write finish attend make

Meg Brooke *has appeared* on television to talk about the Appeal Fund. She *has contacted* the newspapers in order to raise more money for the Fund. Jack Craig *has made* no plans for the immediate future. He (1) __________ a lot of interviews for specialist sailing magazines. That (2) __________ us plenty of good publicity. Rob Adair (3) __________ some new research equipment for the Institute. I (not) (4) __________ him a permanent contract yet because I (5) __________ for the results of the Appeal Fund. Yolanda Richmond (6) __________ the photographs of the expedition to two important international photo agencies. We (already) (7) __________ a large sum of money from the sale. Howard Ellway (8) __________ for forestry posts overseas. He (9) __________ several interesting offers.
Lisa, our research student (still) (10) __________ her thesis. She (11) __________ nearly half of it. My secretary, Suzy, (12) __________ a two-day word-processing course at the local polytechnic. She is now back at work and she (13) __________ the word processor in place of her old electric typewriter.

Exercise 3

Complete this conversation between James and Bill. Then practise it with your partner.

James What's going on (1)__________?
Bill They're (2) __________.
James No one told me about (3) __________.
Bill You're a bit out of touch. Everyone knows that (4) __________.
James That's awful! I (5) __________.
Bill What are you getting so hot under the collar about? That (6) __________ has always been (7) __________.

(1) at the office; across the road

(2) looking for a new manager; building a new shopping centre

(3) the manager; the shopping centre

(4) our boss has joined another company; someone has bought the old supermarket

(5) work in his department; do my shopping there

(6) man; building

(7) a pain in the neck; an eyesore

Exercise 4

How many things in your life have changed recently? Is anything different? Think about these things:

your appearance
your family
the area where you live
your job or the place where you study

Write about these changes and about actions or events that are in progress. Write sentences in the Present Continuous and the Present Perfect tenses, like this:

I've applied for a new job, but I haven't had a reply yet.
We're building an extension to our house.

LESSON 62

They Discovered an Intruder

POLICE REPORT
Officer: Chief Inspector Grenville
Date: 14th May

I was called to the International Ocean Institute, 32 Carlton Square Gardens, SW1 at 23.35 on the night of Friday 14th because local residents had reported a disturbance involving four men at the entrance of the Institute. Two police officers were sent to investigate. All four men were detained at the police station and questioned. Although I have not concluded my investigations, I have reconstructed the events of that night.

At 21.25, three employees of the Institute, Jack Craig, Robert Adair and David Skinner met at the Institute. Next, they went on foot to the nearby Grenadier public house. At 23.15 approximately, they returned to the Institute to collect some belongings. Although they had locked everything before leaving, the door was open. Then, when they entered the Institute office, they discovered an intruder. They pursued the man, Simon Dean, into the street and there was a fight. Finally, several local residents telephoned the police station and the police officers arrived shortly afterwards.

Craig and Dean were arrested, but Craig was released soon afterwards. I have interviewed Dean, a motorcycle messenger from the Grosvenor Express Company. He claims that he entered the Institute to deliver an important package. He says that Dr Geoffrey Walton had given him a key to the Institute. I cannot check his story because I have insufficient evidence so I have asked Sergeant Tucker to make some enquiries on my behalf.

Exercise 1

Inspector Grenville has given Sergeant Tucker his notes. Unfortunately, they're in the wrong order. Read the Police Report and put the notes in the correct order.

a) They ran after the man and a fight started. ____
b) The door of the Institute was open. ____
c) They walked from the Institute to their local pub. ____
d) People who lived nearby telephoned the police. ____
e) They found a man in the Institute office. ____
f) Two police officers arrived. ____
g) Just before half-past nine, Jack, Rob and David met at the Institute. 1
h) They went back to the Institute after they had had a few drinks. ____

Rule: Study these examples.

I can come to see you on Saturday, *but* I can't come to see you on Wednesday.
Although I can come to see you on Saturday, I can't come to see you on Wednesday.
He became a journalist *because* he wanted to meet famous people.
He wanted to meet famous people *so* he became a journalist.

Fill the spaces in the sentences below with 'but', 'although', 'because' or 'so'.

1 I cannot check his story ________ I have insufficient evidence ________ I have asked Sergeant Tucker to make some enquiries.
2 I was called to the Institute ________ local residents had reported a disturbance.
3 ________ they had locked everything before leaving, the door was open.
4 Mr Craig and Mr Dean were arrested, ________ Mr Craig was released soon afterwards.
5 ________ I have not concluded my investigations, I have reconstructed the events of that night.

Exercise 2

Join the following sentences with 'although', 'so', 'but', and 'because'.

1 I'm learning English ________________
2 I still go to the hairdresser regularly ________________
3 I liked the book ________________
4 I saw something suspicious ________________
5 I've got plenty of money ________________
6 I like snakes ________________

a) I don't want to touch them.
b) I didn't like the film of the book.
c) I haven't got much hair.
d) I want to get a job in the export department.
e) It's all in the bank.
f) I called the police.

Can you invent similar sentences about yourself?

Exercise 3

Practise this dialogue with your partner. Then, in pairs, make up similar dialogues. Take turns to be A and B.

A: Hello, is that (1) ________?
B: Yes, can I help you?
A: I'd like to report (2) ________.
B: Can you give me your name and phone number, please?
A: Yes. My name is (Give your name). My number is (Give a telephone number).
B: Where is (3) ________?
A: It's at (Give an address).
B: We'll send (4) ________ right away.

(1) the ambulance service; the police; the fire brigade

(2) an accident; a disturbance; a fire

(3) the accident; the disturbance; the fire

(4) an ambulance; a fire engine; a police car

Exercise 4

Have you ever seen a crime or a fight? Have you read about one recently in the newspaper or heard about one on the radio or television? Make notes from memory about the crime you saw, heard or read about. Put the events in the correct order. Write five sentences to describe the crime. Begin the sentences with these words:

First, ... *Then, ...*
Next, ... *Finally, ...* *After that, ...*

LESSON 63

They'll Have Come to Some Conclusions

Meg Where's Geoffrey?
Jack He's on the phone. He's talking to Inspector Grenville about Simon.
Meg What was Simon doing in the Institute, Jack?
Jack Maybe the police will have found out by now. He wasn't delivering a package. That's for sure!
Meg It's a pity about the fight. It will have earned us a lot of bad publicity. I hope our sponsors don't withdraw their support.
Jack It would be a disaster if they did. Those seven months at sea will all have been a waste of time.
Geoffrey Meg, get your coat. You too, Jack. You're both coming with me. We've got an appointment with Grenville at New Scotland Yard in half an hour.
Meg What's happened?
Geoffrey Well, the police are questioning Simon now and, with a bit of luck, they'll have come to some conclusions by the time we arrive.

*****

Grenville . . . so that's the story. Simon Dean was working for Otto Bergman.
Geoffrey Otto? But I don't understand. He's only a sponsor! He owns a boatyard, that's all.
Jack And he's a diamond smuggler. Sorry, Geoffrey, but I've seen the evidence myself.
Geoffrey I can't believe it! Otto Bergman!
Meg So, Bergman hid the diamonds on the *Ocean Explorer*, and Charles Durberville picked them up when the yacht reached New York.
Grenville Exactly!
Geoffrey What about Simon Dean? Why was he so interested in the Institute?
Grenville His job was to spy on you . . . to inform Bergman of the yacht's movements.
Geoffrey I still don't understand!
Grenville The police arrested Charles Durberville in New York, but Bergman didn't know. He believed Durberville had stolen the diamonds and was on board the *Ocean Explorer*. It was probably a case of mistaken identity. In fact, he thought that Howard Ellway was Charles Durberville.
Jack So Bergman thought we were all working with Durberville and that's why he tried to blow up the yacht.
Meg I expect Bergman will have left the country now that you've caught Simon.
Grenville Well, after Jack told us about the diamonds in Bergman's boatyard, we informed the Portsmouth Police. They sent their officers to the yard and I've just heard that Bergman's been arrested.
Meg Jack.
Jack Yes, Meg. Is something still bothering you?
Meg Do you think Charles looks like Howard?
Jack No . . . but I think Howard looks like Charles.
Meg Thanks a lot, Jack!

Exercise 1

Read the dialogue and find the correct ending to these sentences

1 Simon Dean . . . . . e
2 The fight outside the Institute . . . . . ____
3 If the sponsors withdraw their support . . . . . ____
4 Otto Bergman . . . . . ____
5 Charles Durberville picked up the diamonds . . . . . ____
6 Bergman didn't know . . . . . ____
7 Charles Durberville . . . . . ____
8 Bergman tried to sabotage the expedition . . . . . ____
9 The police arrested Bergman . . . . . ____

a) . . . . . hid his diamonds on the *Ocean Explorer*.
b) . . . . . will have earned the crew a lot of bad publicity.
c) . . . . . those seven months at sea will have been a waste of time.
d) . . . . . looks like Howard Ellway.
e) . . . . . wasn't delivering a package to the Institute.
f) . . . . . that the police had arrested Charles Durberville in New York.
g) . . . . . because he thought the crew were working with Durberville.
h) . . . . . after Jack had told them about the diamonds in his boatyard.
i) . . . . . when the yacht reached New York.

Study the example.

The police *will have found out* by now.

Rule: To show that something will already be completed by a specific time in the future we use the Future Perfect.
The Future Perfect is formed with ________ + ________ + the past participle.

Read the dialogue and fill in the missing words.

1 It ________ us a lot of bad publicity.
2 Bergman ________ the country now that you've caught Simon.
3 Those seven months at sea ________ a waste of time.
4 They ________ to some conclusions by the time we arrive.

Exercise 2

Complete these sentences. Choose from these verbs. Put the verb in the Future Perfect.

publish leave do work repair change start

1 Two weeks from now we ________ our holiday.
2 The film starts at 10.30. You ________ your homework by then.
3 She's always changing her hairstyle. By this time next week she ________ it again.
4 He ________ his book by May.
5 We're late. The plane ________ by the time we arrive at the airport.
6 On 22nd August you ________ for the company for a year.
7 By Friday the workmen ________ our roof.

Exercise 3

Practise this dialogue with your partner. Then, in pairs, make up similar dialogues. Take turns to be A and B.

A: Is something bothering you?
B: I've got an appointment (1) ________ in half an hour.
A: So that's why (2) ________. What is the (3) ________ going to do?
B: With a bit of luck he/she will just give me (4) ________.
A: What if he/she (5) ________?
B: It would be a disaster if he/she did.

(1) at the dentist's; with the principal; with my bank manager

(2) you look so nervous; you've been studying hard; you've been saving money

(3) dentist; principal; bank manager

(4) a check-up; my exam results; some financial advice

(5) takes some of your teeth out; expels you from the college; closes your bank account

Exercise 4

What will you have done by the end of this year? Write three sentences that begin like this:

By the end of this year I will have . . . . .
I expect I will have . . . . .
I hope I will have . . . . .

Interview your partners to find out what they expect and hope they will have done by the end of the year. Write a short report about the most interesting things you have discovered.

LESSON 64

This Would Never Have Happened

Exercise 1

Choose True or False. Then write the sentences from the text that give the answers.

1 Some people sent money after seeing Meg on TV.
2 Before Ranaku arrived they were more than £10 000 short.
3 The Vice Chancellor won't help them if they don't get £500 000.
4 Ranaku gave them more than they needed.
5 Ranaku's government received money from the mining companies.
6 Geoffrey's foot was better.
7 In his short speech, Geoffrey forgot to say that they had made enough money.

Exercise 2

Study the examples.

If Geoff had made a long speech, *he would have bored* everybody.
Did he make a long speech? No.
Did he bore everybody? No.

If the team hadn't helped Ranaku's men, *they wouldn't have defeated* the government.
Did the team help? Yes.
Did they defeat the government? Yes.

This type of 'If' sentence is used when a condition was not completed in the past (sometimes called 'third conditional')
Look at the sentences and finish the rule.

Rule: In the 'If' clause the verb is 'had' + past participle (i.e. the Past Perfect).
In the other clauses the verb form is 'would' + ________ + ________.

Remember that these two verb forms are the same for all persons, eg *I/you/he/she/it/we/they had helped*
I/you/he/she/it/we/they would have defeated

Match the two halves of the sentences.

A

1 If the Institute hadn't raised half a million pounds
2 If Antonia hadn't interviewed Meg
3 If they hadn't gone on their trip
4 If Ranaku hadn't helped them
5 If they hadn't helped Ranaku
6 If Rob hadn't spotted the dolphins
7 If Geoff had made a very long speech

B

a) it would have closed.
b) they wouldn't have reached their target.
c) they wouldn't have had so many cheques.
d) he wouldn't have defeated the government.
e) he would have bored everybody.
f) Yolanda wouldn't have taken any photographs of them.
g) they wouldn't have made £491 025.

Exercise 3

Practise this dialogue with your partner. Then, in pairs, make up similar dialogues. Take turns to be A and B.

A: What would you have done if you hadn't become a (1) sailor.
B: I'd probably have become a (1) journalist.
A: I can't imagine you as a journalist, but you'd have been a good (1) soldier.
B: Oh no! I wouldn't have liked (2) a soldier's life.
A: No, I wouldn't have either.

(1) journalist; soldier; scientist; teacher; racing driver; professional golfer; taxi driver; professional footballer; photographer; hairdresser; dentist; grocer; butcher; priest

(2) a scientist's life; a teacher's life; Etc.

Exercise 4

What wouldn't you have learned about New Zealand, Australia and Nigeria if you hadn't studied *Formula 2*?

REVISION EXERCISES 1

Exercise 1

Write the missing verbs in this conversation between Doug and Pat. Put the verbs in the correct form. Use these verbs:

meet learn speak paint be enjoy study travel

Doug Where are you going?
Pat To the tech. I'm doing a painting course there.
Doug Oh, how long (1) ________ interested in painting?
Pat About a year. I (2) ________ to paint portraits.
Doug How are you getting on?
Pat Fine. I (3) ________ it. Why don't you come too?
Doug To be honest, I'm not interested in (4) ________.
Pat There are lots of other courses. What things do you like?
Doug I like (5) ________.
Pat Well, (6) ________ interested in learning a language? This year there are courses in Greek, Portuguese and Chinese.
Doug I (7) ________ interested in learning Greek, but I don't like (8) ________.
Pat Don't worry. You'll enjoy (9) ________ different people and (10) ________ a new language.

Exercise 2

Suzy is joining a local health club. The receptionist is asking her a lot of questions. Read Suzy's answers and write the receptionist's questions.

Example:
What's your name?
Suzy Small.

1 ______________________________
I was born on 3rd September, 1967.
2 ______________________________
I was born in Reading.
3 ______________________________
I moved to London when I was nine years old.
4 ______________________________
Now I'm twenty-two.
5 ______________________________
At the International Ocean Institute.
6 ______________________________
I've been working there for eleven months.
7 ______________________________
Before that I worked in a bank near my home.

Exercise 3

Hugh and Jennifer got married last month. Since then they've had a few problems. Use the prompts to make sentences about them, like this:

Example:
go to Yugoslavia/get a flight
They wanted to go to Yugoslavia, but they couldn't get a flight.

1. they/drive to the coast/start the car
2. Hugh/thank his relatives for their presents/find their addresses
3. they/eat some Indian food/find an Indian restaurant
4. Jennifer/cook a pizza/find the right ingredients
5. they/take some photographs/understand the camera
6. Hugh/buy a new car/sell his old one
7. they/go camping/find the campsite
8. they/open a bottle of wine/find a corkscrew

Exercise 4

Meg's friend Stephanie used to live in Italy. Three years ago she returned to England. Read about what she *used to do* and what she *does now*. Match the phrases about what Stephanie did in 1981 with those about what she does now. Write sentences like this:

Stephanie used to live in Milan in Italy, but now she lives in Cambridge in England.

1981	Now
travelled to work by car	has a sandwich for lunch at the office
went to a gym twice a week	goes out for a meal with friends or goes to evening classes
went home for lunch	plays tennis three times a week and goes jogging every morning
finished work at 7pm	studies French and Japanese
watched TV in the evenings or went to the cinema	travels to work by bus
studied Italian	finishes work at 5pm

Exercise 5

Using the information below, write a short report about these students at the Anglo Institute.

Name	Job	From	To
Franco	photographer	1980	now
Gabriella	student	1984	1986
Alessandra	accountant	1987	1988
Marcos	sales manager	1983	now
Fabrice	clerk	1984	1989
Gerard	graphic designer	1985	now
Cristina	doctor	1987	now

Write sentences like this:

Franco has been a photographer for ten years. Gabriella was a student for two years. Alessandra . . .

Now write about people in your family in the same way.

REVISION EXERCISES 2

Exercise 1

Match the sentences.

1 Here are the books.
2 Don't forget the report.
3 I can't find the shoes.
4 The horse is tired.
5 The cassette is mine.
6 The bedroom is beautiful.

a) I wore *them* yesterday.
b) You painted *it* last year.
c) I ordered *them* from the bookshop.
d) Yolanda heard *it* yesterday.
e) You wrote *it* yesterday.
f) I rode *him* yesterday.

Now join the sentences with 'that', but leave out the word in italics.

Example:

Here are the books that I ordered from the bookshop.

In all the sentences you have joined, 'that' is the object. When 'that' is the object it is often omitted, especially in speaking.

Repeat your sentences, omitting 'that'.

Exercise 2

Complete the sentences, changing the verb as necessary.

1 Mr and Mrs Lewis will go around the world when Mr Lewis (retire).
2 I'll go to bed as soon as the programme (finish).
3 Lindy will change her hair style when she (get) older.
4 Meg will telephone as soon as she (arrive) in New York.
5 We'll eat as soon as the dinner (be) ready.
6 Daniel will join the police when he (leave) school.
7 I'll buy a new car when I (get) more money.
8 Mary will write a letter when she (have) enough time.

Exercise 3

Finish the sentences in any way you want to.

Example:
When ________, I'll go home.
When the lesson finishes, I'll go home.

1 I'll go for a long holiday when ________.
2 I'll feel very sad when ________.
3 When ________, I'll kiss them all.
4 I'll have something to drink as soon as ________.
5 I'll be very happy when ________.
6 The bus will leave as soon as ________.

Exercise 4

Give these people some advice. Tell them what they should or shouldn't do.

Example:
Simon is cold. He should wear a coat.

1 John has a high temperature.
2 Susan's boyfriend has left her.
3 My car won't start.
4 I am very hungry.
5 David has no friends.
6 Pierre wants to learn English.
7 Carol feels very unhappy.
8 Carlos has got no money.

Exercise 5

In a public park you should think about other people. Don't play your radio loudly. Control your dog. You should also be careful. Put your wallet or bag in a safe place. Now look at the picture and say what the people should or should not do.

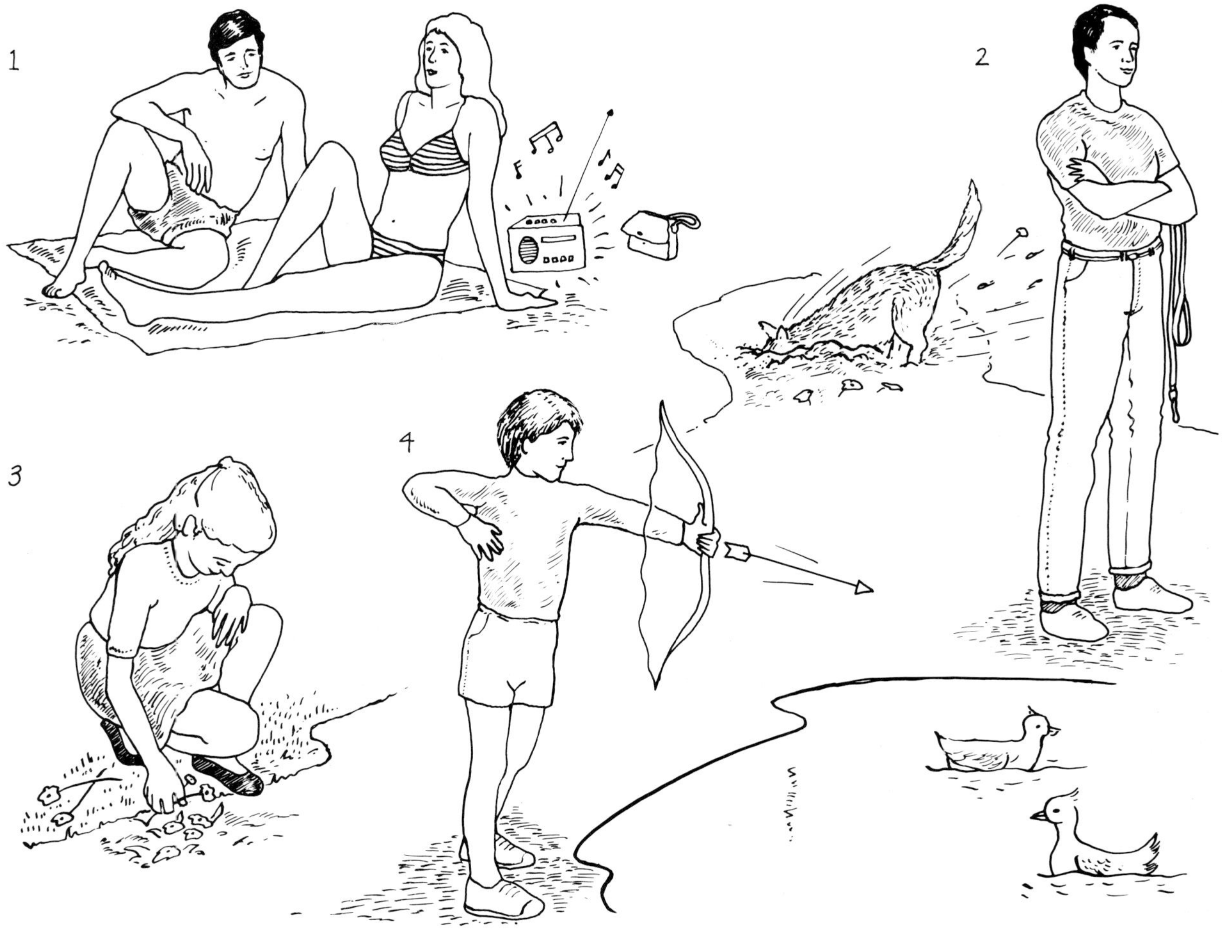

Exercise 6

Remember what Maria said:

'Pete left me. He had met someone else.'

Janet is waiting for Lindy at the cinema. Complete the conversation by putting the verbs in brackets into the Past Simple or the Past Perfect.

Janet You're late!
Lindy Sorry! I (run) to the bus stop. The bus (go), so I walked.
Janet It doesn't matter. I (arrive) early, but they (sell) all the tickets.
Lindy So let's go to Al's Bar and talk to a few friends.
Janet Well, I (go) there last night at this time and it was empty. Everybody (go) home.
Lindy But it's only 8 o'clock!

REVISION EXERCISES 3

Exercise 1

Write sentences comparing the things given in the circle.

Example:

Jogging is safer than mountain climbing.
Mountain climbing is more exciting than swimming.

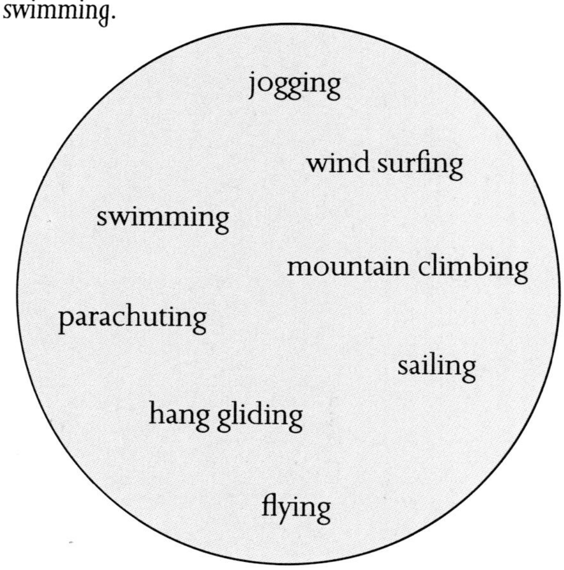

Then make lists of other things and write sentences comparing pairs of items.

Exercise 2

Change the verbs below into the Present Continuous and put them into the correct gaps in the passage.

Example:

Verb: practise
Present Continuous: *is practising*

Nowadays, Lisa (1) ________ a very busy life. This month, she (2) ________ evening classes. She (3) ________ to cook Indian food. She also wants to learn word processing, so she (4) ________ on a word processor at the office. She (5) ________ on her dissertation. She (6) ________ microscopic marine organisms. Meanwhile, at home, she (7) ________ some new clothes.

practise	study	lead
learn	attend	work
make		

Exercise 3

Here are some statements. Are they true or false?

1 Charles Durberville has been looking for a new position for some time.
2 Howard Ellway has been working as a forestry consultant for two years.
3 Howard has been sailing for ten years.
4 Queen Elizabeth has been sitting on the throne of England since 1960.
5 The Eiffel Tower has been standing in Paris for over a hundred years.
6 Men have been exploring space since 1970.
7 Concorde has been flying to New York for twenty years.
8 You have been learning English for ten years.

Now make up six sentences like these. They can be true or false. Read them to a partner. Your partner will say if the sentences are true or false.

Exercise 4

Finish the sentences in column 1 by choosing from column 2.

1	2
1 If a car runs out of petrol,	**a)** I'll be sick.
2 If there isn't any wind,	**b)** it will leak.
3 If you stick a pin into a paper cup,	**c)** the sea will be rough.
4 If there's a storm,	**d)** it won't start.
5 If the sea is rough,	**e)** the yacht won't move.

Now make up a similar set of sentences in two columns. Mix the order of the items in column 2. Give the sentences to a partner to finish.

Exercise 5

Write about some things and places in your town, like this:

The cathedral is the oldest building and the duke's palace is the most beautiful. The tallest building is the new business centre. The most expensive restaurant is 'Le Petit Blanc', but the cheapest is 'Le Petit Tonneau'.

REVISION EXERCISES 4

Exercise 1

Write the correct comparative or superlative forms of these adjectives in the sentences below.

expensive famous exciting difficult strong athletic fantastic delicious disappointing

1 We have many good players in the football team, but Howard is *the strongest* and ________.
2 When they told me I hadn't got the job, it was ________ moment of my life.
3 Robert thinks Paris is exciting, but New York is ________.
4 These hamburgers are delicious, but the ones in the restaurant next door are even ________.
5 The salt beef sandwiches at Bloom's are ________ than the ones at Harveys's Deli.
6 Yolanda took Robert to some of ________ places in New York.
7 Learning a European langauge is difficult, but learning to speak Chinese is even ________.
8 Jack's just come back from the Caribbean and he has ________ tan I've ever seen.

Exercise 2

Write five things you are going to do next week. Work in pairs and ask questions like this:

You What are you going to do on Sunday morning?
Your partner I'm going to drive to the coast with some friends. What are you going to do on Sunday morning?
You I haven't decided yet.
Your partner What are you going to do on Monday evening?
You I'm going to prepare for my English test.

When you've finished, write a short report about what you and your partner are going to do during the week. Write sentences like this:

On Sunday morning, Nathalie is going to drive to the coast with some friends. On Monday evening I'm going to prepare for my English test.

Exercise 3

Use the endings below to finish sentences 1–8. Not all the endings are correct.

1 Leave the house at 9.00am ________
2 Post my letters ________
3 If you're thirsty, ________
4 Take a taxi ________
5 If you're not doing anything on Friday, ________
6 Give Stuart my regards ________
7 Buy yourself a sandwich ________
8 I'll buy you a drink tonight ________

a) Pat makes you a cup of tea.
b) if you went out early.
c) if you are hungry.
d) if your interview is at 10.00am.
e) we go to the cinema.
f) if you get the job.
g) we'll go to the cinema.
h) if you see him.
i) if you go out early.
j) Pat will make you a cup of tea.
k) if the buses are full.
l) if your interview was at 10.00am.

Exercise 4

Here are some reported questions. What were these people's actual words?

Example:

Nigel asked if Stephanie was nearly ready?
Nigel *Is Stephanie nearly ready?*

1 David asked if Tricia was at home.
David ________
2 Cinzia asked the taxi driver if he could take her to Blackford Road.
Cinzia ________
3 Maureen asked if Ian was collecting her at the station?
Maureen ________
4 Antonio asked the newspaper man if he had got change of a £10 note?
Antonio ________
5 Roger asked if he could use our phone.
Roger ________
6 Kumiko asked if this was the right stop.
Kumiko ________

Exercise 5

Practise the dialogue with a partner. Take turns at being A and B.

A: Do you think (1) it will rain tomorrow?
B: No, I don't think so. (2) It was fine today. What do you think?
A: (3) It may rain. (4) The weather forecast wasn't very good.
B: Well, in that case, I may (5) take my umbrella with me tomorrow. Will (6) there be room for it in your bag?
A: I think so. Anyway, (7) I may take a larger bag.

(1) there will be a train strike tomorrow/that actor will be in the play next week/there will be an English test tomorrow
(2) There's nothing in the newspaper/The critics didn't like him/There was a test last week
(3) There may be a strike/He may leave the play/We may have a test
(4) The radio news bulletin/His acting/Our class's last test
(5) take a taxi/book some new theatre tickets/do some revision tonight
(6) we have enough money for the journey/we be able to get some/you have time before you go out
(7) I may stop at the bank before we leave/I may book some opera seats instead/I may stay at home tonight

REVISION EXERCISES 5

Exercise 1

Remember:

Howard (to Rob) 'Get a bucket!'
Howard told Rob *to get* a bucket.

Meg (to Howard) 'Don't argue!'
Meg told Howard *not to argue.*

Change the following commands into reported commands.

1 **The policeman** (to the driver): 'Stop!'
2 **Mrs Lewis** (to her son John): 'Do your homework!'
3 **Mr Jones** (to Mrs Jones): 'Drive more slowly!'
4 **The manager** (to the secretary): 'Don't be late!'
5 **Mrs Wilkins** (to her little boy): 'Don't run across the road!'

Exercise 2

Think of five things you told people to do or not to do last week, and report them, eg: *I told my mother to go to the doctor.*

Exercise 3

Give answers to the following questions, as in the example, using the best word from the list.

Example:

Why can't Maria do the exercise quickly?
It's too difficult to do quickly.

1 Why can't Philip lift the box?
2 Why doesn't Ann eat her curry?
3 Why doesn't Jacques buy a flat in Paris?
4 Why doesn't John finish his homework quickly?
5 Why doesn't Janet take her baby to the cinema?

difficult young expensive heavy hot

Exercise 4

Complete the following passage with 'some of' or 'all of'.

Jane had a party last Friday because it was her birthday. She invited (1) ________ her friends, but only (2) ________ them came. She prepared a lot of food, and (3) ________ it was eaten. Jane is an excellent cook. They had a lot to drink, and they had a cake. It had 25 candles, but Jane managed to blow out (4) ________ them. Then (5) ________ her friends sang 'Happy Birthday' very loudly. (6) ________ them left at eleven because they had to work on Saturday morning, but many of them stayed until two o'clock.

Exercise 5

Give these people advice, by choosing a phrase from those given.

Example:

John needs more exercise. He goes everywhere by car!
If I were John, I'd go to work by bicycle.

1 Albert can't see very well these days.
(go to a doctor/an optician/a dentist)
2 Jane left her handbag on the train.
(go to the police/forget about it/go to the lost property office)
3 Mario is poor, but his girlfriend Alicia wants him to buy an expensive car.
(buy a cheap car/leave Alicia/try to get a better job)
4 Daniel wants promotion in his company, but his English isn't good enough.
(go on holiday to England/join an evening class/watch English films)
5 Mary lives in London. She wants a quiet holiday.
(go camping near Nice/go to a cottage in Scotland/go to a hotel in Sweden)

Exercise 6

Read the descriptions of the four people below. Then read the extract from Lanchester's Weekend Diary, and say two things that each person might do.

Roger Vickers: A retired schoolteacher; he doesn't drink or smoke; he likes classical music, reading, walking.

Maryse Simon: A French au pair, aged 24. She wants to improve her English. She's interested in English traditions and songs; she plays the guitar.

Kevin Brown: He works as an assistant in a video shop; he likes drinking beer, football, fast cars and pop music. He's 22.

Ann Marconi: Aged 35; she is the manageress of a large and successful fashion store. She's very keen on fashion and clothes. She has very little free time, but likes the cinema.

Lanchester Weekend Diary – Friday 3rd May

THEATRE
Lanchester Amateur Dramatic Society: 'The Tempest' by Shakespeare 8.00 at the St Mary's Hall (tickets £3.00)

CINEMA
AB Cinema: 'Born to Kill' (action-packed war film) 19.00 and 23.00 (£4.00 and £5.00)

FILM CLUB Festival of Russian Films 'Battleship Potemkin' 20.00 (£1.50 members: £2.50 non-members)

LECTURES
English Poetry of the Sixteenth Century: Professor Beck (Library: free entry) 19.00

CLUBS
Rockets: Lanchester's liveliest club. Tonight the spectacular new group *Stax*. (entrance £4.00; last entry 10.30)
The Hub: good food till midnight; with Anna Zeiler's sophisticated 20s style cabaret (entrance £10.00)

PUBS
The Sun: An evening of folksongs with the Taylor Brothers
The Red Lion: For a pleasant evening with good beer and a traditional atmosphere with Ron and Ann

FOOTBALL
Lanchester v. Burnside (19.30) Lanchester Stadium

REVISION EXERCISES 6

Exercise 1

Complete the story below with the correct Past Tense and Past Perfect forms of these verbs. The verbs are in the wrong order for the story. (The verbs are used more than once.)

stop	crash	telephone	survive
contact	continue	stay	put
go	cut	slam	want
start	pack	repair	

Last week we (1) ________ to visit friends in York. Unfortunately, although our journey (2) ________ well, it (3) ________ not ________ well.
We (4) ________ early and (5) ________ on the motorway. About half way to York, a truck (6) ________ into us. We (7) ________ at some road works. The truck (8) ________ into the back of our car. I (9) ________ myself on some broken glass. Fortunately, we (10) ________ a first aid kit in the car, so I (11) ________ some sticking plaster on the cut. We (12) ________ the Automobile Association, and they (13) ____ a garage which (14) ________ the damage. But, we (15) ________ not ________ to continue our journey, so we (16) ________ our friends in York. So, although we (17) ________ the accident, we (18) ________ not ________ to York after all

Exercise 2

Read the passage and then put the verbs below into the Past Passive and write them in the appropriate blanks in the text.

inspect	ask	hide	tell
reprimand	stop	interrogate	
find	call	turn	

Did I tell you about the time I (1) ________ by the customs? It was very unpleasant. When I was coming through the green channel, I (2) ______ to open my luggage. I (3) ________ and everything (4) ________ upside down. I was very worried and didn't really pay attention. To my horror, some diamonds (5) ________ in my suitcase. Then I (6) ________ by an officer. I (7) ________ that I was under arrest. I was very worried. I asked to speak to a lawyer. A lawyer (8) ________. He asked to see the suitcase. Although it was exactly the same as mine, it wasn't my case! The customs (9) ________ for arresting me. But, meanwhile, the real smuggler had escaped with my suitcase!

Exercise 3

Respond to the situations below as in the example using 'should have' or 'shouldn't have'.

Example:

Fred had an exam last Monday. He stayed out late at a party on Sunday.
He shouldn't have stayed out late.

1 Mandy is slimming. She ate three large meals last week.
2 Mark didn't stop at a red traffic light. He hit an old man.
3 Mr Brown didn't lock his door and someone stole his television.
4 John played his records too loudly and woke the neighbour's baby.
5 Nancy stayed out in the sun too long and got badly sunburnt.

Exercise 4

Report the following dialogue, using where appropriate the pattern:

X wondered if . . .

Example:

Yolanda Is Rob on board?
Meg I think he is.
Yolanda wondered if Rob was on board. Meg thought he was.

Lisa Is Rob coming to the yacht club?
Jack I don't know.
Meg Is he on duty?
Lisa No, he isn't.
Jack Is Yolanda coming, as well?
Lisa Yes, I think she is.
Jack Is she taking us to her favourite nightspot?
Meg I hope she is!

Exercise 5

Complete this story by adding 'a good deal of' or 'a good many of' in the appropriate spaces in the text.

We had (1) ________ trouble when we arrived at our holiday home. (2) ________ the windows were broken. (3) ________ the kitchen equipment was missing. (4) ________ my books were torn. Fortunately, there was (5) ________ wine in the cellar. So, we opened some bottles and we drank (6) ________ it. After that, we felt much better.

REVISION EXERCISES 7

Exercise 1

Example:

I don't like fish. Today we're having fish for lunch.
I wish we weren't having fish for lunch.

1 Terri takes a size 16 dress. The dress in the shop is only in size 12.
Terri wishes ______________________

2 Frank got 55 out of 100 for his maths test. He needed to get 70 out of 100.
Frank ______________________

3 Lucy would like a video recorder, but she doesn't have one.
Lucy ______________________

4 Peter is always arguing with his wife. It was a mistake for him to marry her.
Peter ______________________

5 I don't like short hair. I've got short hair myself, but I think long hair is more attractive.
I ______________________

6 Mike and Dave don't earn much money. They'd like to earn more.
Mike and Dave ______________________

Exercise 2

This chart gives the performances of three students, Graham, David and Paul in three sports events over a period of two years. Study the chart and complete the sentences.

Name	Age	100 Metres	High jump	Javelin
Graham	21	16.0 seconds	2 metres 10 cms	44 metres 80 cms
	23	15.0 seconds	2 metres 30 cms	46 metres
David	18	15.5 seconds	2 metres 40 cms	43 metres 30 cms
	20	16.5 seconds	2 metres 50 cms	47 metres
Paul	22	14.5 seconds	2 metres 20 cms	46 metres
	24	15.0 seconds	2 metres 35 cms	49 metres 10 cms

Examples:

When he was *twenty-one*, Graham *could jump* 2 metres 10 cms.
David *could run 100 metres* in 16.5 seconds when he was *twenty*.
When he was *twenty-one*, Graham *could throw* the javelin 44 metres 80 cms.

1 When he was twenty, David __________ 2 metres 50 cms.

2 Paul __________ in 14.5 seconds when he was twenty-two.

3 Graham __________ 2 metres 30 cms when he was __________.

4 When David was eighteen, he __________ the javelin __________.

5 When he was __________, Graham __________ in 16.0 seconds.

6 Paul __________ the javelin 49 metres 10 cms when he was __________.

Exercise 3

Use the endings (**a** to **h**) to complete sentences 1 to 8.

Example:

If I lost my keys I'd borrow my neighbour's ladder and climb through a window.

1 If a shop assistant was rude to me ______________________

2 I would speak to my best friend ______________________

3 If there were no trains ______________________

4 I'd be very angry if ______________________

5 If the painting on my wall was worth £1500 ______________________

6 My friends would help me if ______________________

7 If I had to leave my home town ______________________

8 I'd go to the hospital if ______________________

a) I'd catch a bus instead.
b) someone borrowed my car without asking me.
c) I'd look after it more carefully.
d) if I needed advice.
e) I'd complain to the manager.
f) I'd be very unhappy.
g) I broke my leg.
h) they could.

Exercise 4

This is Bill's first day at Parker's Department Store. When Sybil the Manageress returns from lunch, she has to sort out all Bill's problems at the shop's Information Desk. What does Bill tell her? Complete the conversation.

Sybil Were there any inquiries when I went to lunch?
Bill Yes, lots. All these people are waiting to ask you something.
Sybil What does the tall woman want?
Bill She's *the one who wants a radio for her car.*
Sybil What about the man with the glasses?
Bill He's (1) ______________________
Sybil What's this parcel?
Bill Oh, that's (2) ______________________
Sybil And what's this hairdryer doing here?
Bill That's (3) __________ and the woman over there with the dog is (4) ______________________.
Sybil Who's the girl with the blonde hair?
Bill She's the secretary (5) ______________________
Sybil Does the man with the moustache want the stationery department too?
Bill No, he's the foreign gentleman (6) ______________________
Sybil Is that everything? Where did this leather glove come from?
Bill That's a (7) ______________________

Can you answer this question?

Who owns the leather glove?
It probably belongs to ______________________

Exercise 5

Dave's birthday was last week. There were lots of last minute preparations for his party. Here are the notes that Suzy made before the party.

Her friends managed to do some things but not others. Make sentences like this:

Debbie managed to make a cake.
John didn't manage to hire the glasses.

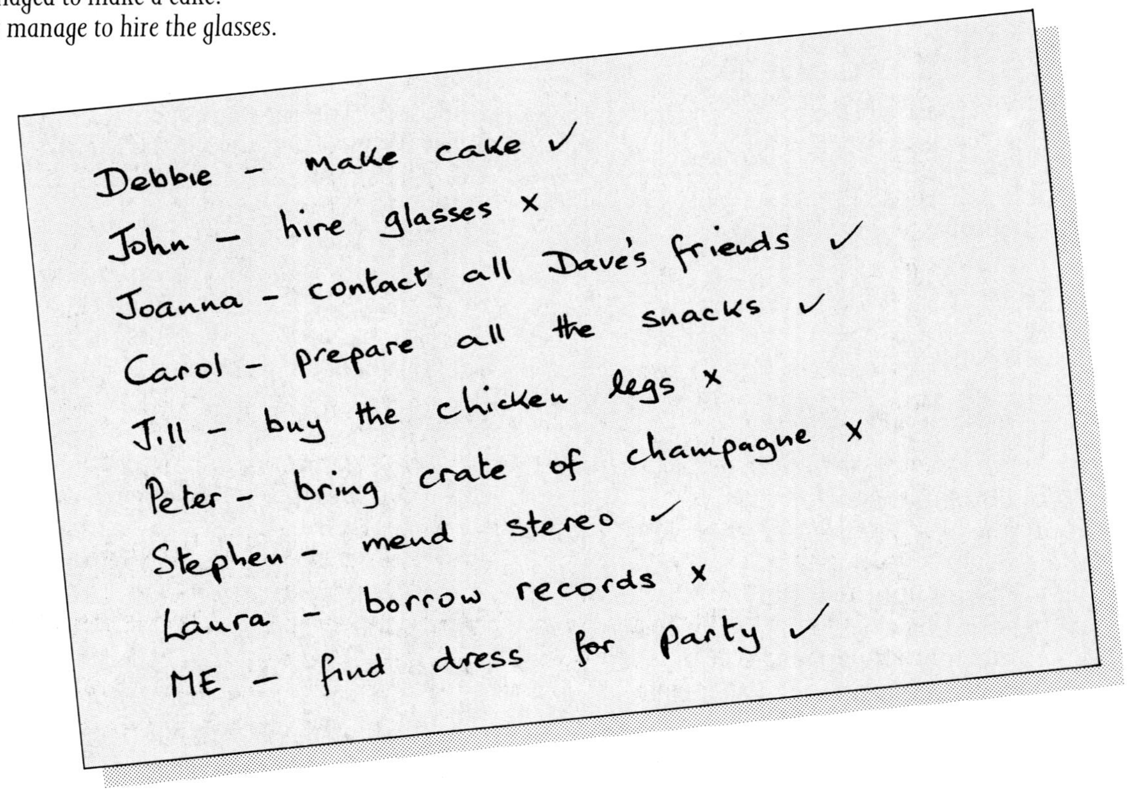

Exercise 6

Michael Vincent was asked by his doctor to fill in a questionnaire.
Here is the completed questionnaire.

Do you take regular exercise?	*Not usually.*
Do you drink coffee?	*Yes, always.*
Do you sleep well at night?	*Yes, normally.*
Do you eat green vegetables?	*Sometimes.*
Do you digest food well?	*No, often very badly.*
Do you stay up late at night?	*Not often.*
Do you fall asleep during the day?	*Frequently.*

Complete the doctor's report using the information from the questionnaire.

Mr Vincent *normally sleeps well* at night. He (1) ________ regular exercise. He (2) ________ green vegetables, but he (3) ________ food (4) ________. He (5) ________ coffee, but he (6) ________ during the day. He (7) ________ up late at night.

REVISION EXERCISES 8

Exercise 1

Use 'Would you like . . .' to make a polite offer for these situations. Choose from the list to help make your offer.

Example:

Your friend looks very thirsty.
Would you like a drink?

1 Your friend looks very tired.
2 John looks hungry.
3 A friend is staying with you. You think her room is cold.
4 Mary must get to the town centre quickly.
5 You think your friend's gin and tonic is not very cold.

something to eat; a rest; a lift in my car; an electric fire; some ice

Exercise 2

Remember:

If Rob passed the exam his mother *would* be happy. (quite certain)
If Rob passed the exam he *might* move to London. (uncertain)

What would/might you do in the following situations? Use an 'if' sentence with a modal verb (*would* or *might*) as above. The first three are started for you:

Situations

1 You feel ill on an aeroplane. (*If I felt ill on an aeroplane, I would/might . . . .*)
2 You find a wallet full of money in the street. (*If I found a wallet full of money in the street, I would/might . . . .*)
3 You leave your bag in a taxi. (*If I left my bag in a taxi . . . .*)
4 In a busy street, you see a pickpocket taking an old lady's purse.
5 At the end of a flight, your luggage is not in the airport.
6 You win an enormous amount of money in a lottery.
7 You see a strange object flying in the sky.
8 One night you are alone in your house and you hear a strange noise outside the door.
9 You arrange to meet a friend at his house. You go to the house but nobody is at home.
10 You wake up one Monday morning feeling very depressed and tired. You don't want to go to work.

Exercise 3

Remember: You use 'with' for physical characteristics or things that people carry eg '*the girl with red hair*', '*the girl with an umbrella*'; 'in' for things people wear eg '*the girl in a red dress*'.

Look at the drawings and identify the people, using the same pattern as in the example.

Example:
The man with curly hair is called Bob.

Useful phrases:
a long beard; curly hair; straight hair; a suitcase
a long dress; shorts; a sari

Exercise 4

Match the sentences to the situations. The first one is done for you.

1 I arrived late at the station, but the train was delayed.
2 A tree fell on Tim's car, but he wasn't in it.
3 We went for a picnic in the country, but it rained all day.
4 Bill's car broke down, but his friend Jane saw him and stopped her car.

a) It's lucky he wasn't in it.
b) It's a pity it rained.
c) It's lucky the train was delayed.
d) It's lucky she saw him.

REVISION EXERCISES 9

Exercise 1

Practise this dialogue with a partner. Take turns to be A and B.

A: What's the matter? Why haven't you (1) finished the repairs?
B: We can't (2) repair anything (3) until they bring the tools.
A: That's a nuisance. We can't wait until they (3) bring the tools.
B: Well, I'm afraid you'll have to.

(1) bought the tickets
gone for a drive
had dinner
prepared the report.

(2) buy anything
go anywhere
eat anything
prepare anything

(3) come with the money
deliver the car
return with the food
bring the information

Exercise 2

Complete the text with the following:

everyone anyone, no one someone
nothing something anything

We had a problem. ________ agreed to do ________, but ________ did ________. Everyone thought that ________ else was doing ________, and ________ checked to find out if ________ was doing ________. As a result, ________ was done. Everyone was very surprised when ________ was ready. There is a lesson in this. If ________ is to do ________, then ________ must do one thing. If ________ does anything, ________ gets done.

Exercise 3

Complete the following passage, using the Present Continuous Passive.

We visited my old village the other day. Unfortunately, it is changing a lot and in a few years, nothing will be left. The old houses (1) turn into flats, the gardens (2) destroy, the old town square (3) turn into a car park, the cinema (4) make into a supermarket, the forest (5) cut down, factories (6) build and the lake (7) polluted. It's a disaster!

Exercise 4

Here are some sentences about what people do now. Make up sentences about what they used to do in the past.

Example:

They live in suburbs of large towns. (small villages)
They used to live in small villages.

1 They live in apartments. (houses)
2 They work in factories and offices. (on farms)
3 They go to work by car. (by bus)
4 They have two holidays a year. (one holiday)
5 They have colour television. (black and white television)
6 They shop in supermarkets once a week. (at the market)
7 They dine out once or twice a month. (once or twice a year)
8 They have very small families. (large families)

Write about the way people used to live in your town or country.

REVISION EXERCISES 10

Exercise 1

Complete the dialogue with these words. They can be used more than once.
someone somewhere anywhere anyone everywhere

A: What have you lost?
B: My (1) purse. I can't find it ________.
A: Well, it must be ________ in this room.
B: It isn't. I've looked ________.
A: Are you sure? Think carefully. Is there ________ that you haven't looked?
B: No, there isn't. I think ________ has taken it.
A: Did ________ come in here this morning? Perhaps ________ came in while you were out of the (2) office?
B: The (3) sandwich man came while I was (4) filing some papers.
A: Well, I expect you've looked ________, but not in (5) the filing cabinet.

Now practise the dialogue with your partner. Make different dialogues using the words below.

(1) wallet/ring/watch
(2) house/bank
(3) delivery man/milkman/security man
(4) putting away my tools/packing the freezer/ counting some money
(5) your tool box/the deep freeze/the safe

Exercise 2

Rob doesn't often eat porridge, but he knows how it's made. Follow the pictures to find out how to make perfect porridge.

(a)
First . . .

(b)
Then . . .

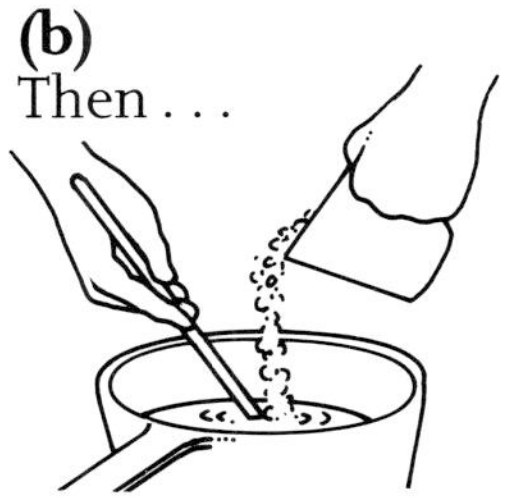

(c)
Next . . .

(d)
After that . . .

(e)
Then . . .

(f)
After that . . .

(g)
Finally . . .

Using the pictures to guide you, put these instructions into the correct order.

1 ____ Add a pinch of salt.
2 ____ Turn down the heat.
3 ____ Pour three cups of cold milk into a saucepan.
4 ____ Serve the porridge and sprinkle it with a little sugar.
5 ____ Stir one cup of oats into the milk.
6 ____ Bring the mixture to the boil.
7 ____ Allow the oats to simmer and cook for five minutes.

Now re-write the instructions using the Present Passive voice. Begin your sentences with the sequences from the pictures above. (First, then, next, etc.)

Rob's recipe for perfect porridge

a) *First, three cups of cold milk are poured into a saucepan.*
b) *Then,* ________________________
c) ________________________
d) ________________________
e) ________________________
f) ________________________
g) ________________________

Exercise 3

Match these phrases (**a** to **h**) with the sentences 1 to 8 below and make sentences with 'had better' (*'d better*) or 'would rather' (*'d rather*).

a) contact the passport office
b) go to the doctor
c) live in the country
d) hide the fragments
e) have a cup of tea
f) visit Los Angeles
g) watch a tennis match
h) stay at her mother's house tonight

Examples:

1 Rob feels ill. (b) *He'd better go to the doctor.*
2 She's given me a cup of black coffee. (e) *I'd rather have a cup of tea.*
3 Howard dislikes cities. ____________
4 Suzy's forgotten her keys. ____________
____
5 Meg's not keen on Florida. ____________
____
6 Rob's going to a rugby match with Yolanda.
____
____
7 Dave's lost his passport. ____________
____
8 Geoffrey's broken Dorothy's favourite vase.
____
____

Exercise 4

A Write about your own preferences, using the words below.

Example:

swimming/tennis
I like playing tennis, but I'd rather go swimming.

1 home/a party
2 Italian food/French food
3 plane/train
4 the seaside/the countryside
5 milk/orange juice

Now ask your partner about his or her preferences. Make questions like this:
Would you rather go swimming or play tennis?

B Invent five problems and write them on a piece of paper.

Example:

I've got toothache.
I don't know anyone.

Tell your problems to your partner. Your partner should give you advice like this:

You'd better make an appointment at the dentist's.
You'd better join a social club.

Now give your partner advice about his or her problems.

Exercise 5

Complete these sentences as in the examples.

Examples:

We *would have chosen* the Vietnamese restaurant if it *had been* cheaper.
(choose/be)

If I *had not answered* the phone, I *wouldn't have been* late for work.
(not answer/not be)

1 You ________ that job if she ________ a good reference for you.
(get/write)
2 He ________ German if he ________ in Switzerland.
(not learn/not work)
3 If I ________ her again, I ________ her name.
(meet/find out)
4 She ________ that book if we ________ her a copy.
(not read/not give)
5 I ________ by now if she ________ talking.
(finish/stop)
6 If I ________ a degree in engineering, I ________ the job.
(not have/not get)
7 ________ you ________ to the party if she ________ you?
(go/invite)

REVISION EXERCISES 11

Exercise 1

Remember:

'So . .' agrees with an affirmative statement:
eg *'I like wine.'* *'So do I.'*

Auxiliaries:

'Jane's hungry.' *'So is Bill.'*
'I've seen the film.' *'So has my brother.'*

'Neither . . .' agrees with a negative statement:
eg *'I don't like beer.'* *'Neither does John.'*

Auxiliaries:
'I can't play the piano.' *'Neither can Michael.'*
'Jack isn't playing.' *'Neither is John.'*

Read the descriptions of Marina, Yasuko and Pascale.

	Marina	**Yasuko**	**Pascale**
Drives a car	Yes	Yes	No
Lives in a flat	No	Yes	Yes
Works in an office	Yes	No	Yes
Hobbies	tennis, dancing, reading	reading, riding, listening to pop music	dancing, listening to pop music
Family	two sisters one brother	one sister one brother	one sister one brother
Boyfriend	No	Yes	No

Now agree with the statements, using 'so' or 'neither'. The first is done for you.

1. Marina can drive. *So can Yasuko.*
2. Yasuko lives in a flat.
3. Pascale works in an office.
4. Yasuko doesn't like tennis.
5. Pascale likes listening to pop music.
6. Marina doesn't like riding.
7. Yasuko likes reading.
8. Pascale hasn't got two brothers.
9. Marina has got one brother.
10. Marina hasn't got a boyfriend.

(**Note:** If you want to disagree, you usually use 'But . . .')
eg *'Marina has got two sisters.'* *'But Pascale hasn't.'*
'Pascale doesn't like tennis.' *'But Marina does.'*

Exercise 2

Remember:

This pattern is often used to show that a decision has already been made.
If Sally goes to LA, she's flying British Airways.

Match the two halves of the sentence.

1 If John goes to New York
2 If we go to Ray's Restaurant
3 If I buy a new car
4 If I go to Tunisia this year
5 If we go by train

a) I'm getting the latest Peugeot.
b) I'm going to visit the desert.
c) he's flying Pan Am.
d) we're not going second class.
e) nobody's ordering the pizza.

Exercise 3

Example:

The car was very expensive. I couldn't buy it.
The car was too expensive for me to buy.

Imagine you had a very bad meal in a restaurant, and change the following sentences in the same way:

1 The martini was very strong. I couldn't drink it.
2 The soup was very cold. I couldn't eat it.
3 The food was very salty. I couldn't eat it.
4 The meat was very tough. I couldn't cut it.
5 The wine was very sweet. I couldn't drink it.
6 The cheese was very strong. I couldn't eat it.
7 The coffee was very weak. I couldn't drink it.
8 The bill was very high. I couldn't pay it.

Exercise 4

Mary has left a note for her husband John. Complete it by putting in the phrasal verbs from the list given.

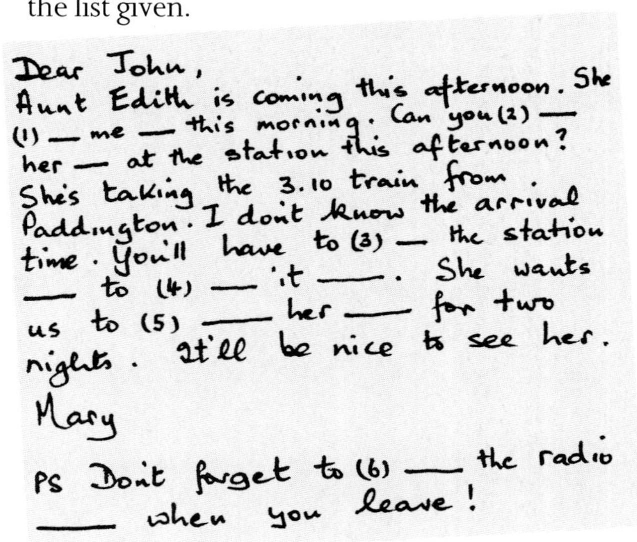

Dear John,
Aunt Edith is coming this afternoon. She (1) — me — this morning. Can you (2) — her — at the station this afternoon? She's taking the 3.10 train from Paddington. I don't know the arrival time. You'll have to (3) — the station — to (4) — it —. She wants us to (5) — her — for two nights. It'll be nice to see her.

Mary

PS Don't forget to (6) — the radio — when you leave!

Verbs
pick . . . up; switch . . . off; phone . . . up; put . . . up; find . . . out

Exercise 5

Respond to sentences 1–8 using 'must' or 'should'.

Remember:

Must is very strong (necessity).
Should is less strong (obligation).

1 John wants to work in France. (speak French)
2 I want to take more exercise. (go jogging)
3 I want to travel to the USA. (have a valid passport)
4 What happens when the traffic lights are red? (the cars – stop)
5 What does this sign mean?

(not – smoke)

6 What does this sign mean?

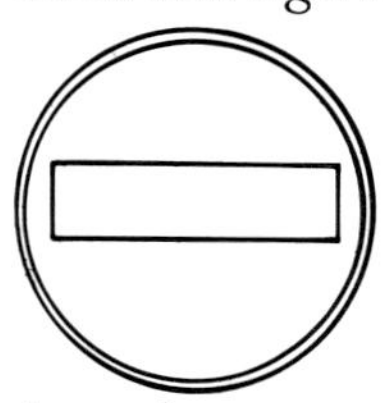

(not – enter)

7 What does this sign mean?

(drive – carefully)

8 What does this sign mean?

(not drive more than 30 miles per hour)

REVISION EXERCISES 12

Exercise 1

Report these promises, using the two patterns:

X promised to + verb

Howard promised to telephone the suppliers.

X promised noun/pronoun + that + pronoun + verb

Howard promised Meg that he would telephone the suppliers.

1 **Jack** I'll repair the damage as soon as possible.
2 **Howard** Meg, I'll take you to dinner on Saturday night.
3 **Lisa** Yolanda, I'll bake a cake for Jack's birthday.
4 **Yolanda** Lisa, I'll take your photograph in the morning.
5 **Rob** I'll send a message to Geoff at once.
6 **Meg** Rob, I'll get a new battery for the radio.
7 **Suzy** Dorothy, I'll hide Geoff's cigarettes.
8 **Yolanda** I'll contact the press agency on Tuesday.

Exercise 2

Change these verbs into the Past Simple tense.

deliver	go	promise
arrive	leave	stay
pay	meet	visit
drive	have	finish

Then use the Past Simple verbs in a story. Use the verbs in any order, and use each verb at least once. Compare your story with what other people in the class have written.

Exercise 3

Use these adjectives where appropriate in the sentences below. Some can be used more than once.

disappointing
captivating
infuriating
terrifying
interesting
exciting
fascinating

1 The weather was cold and wet. The food was poor. Altogether, we found the place very ________.
2 At times he can be ________. He's always late. He never finishes on time. I'm fed up with the way he behaves.
3 Last night we went to see that new horror film. It really was quite ________. I couldn't sleep after seeing it.
4 We went to the museum of rural life the other day. It's full of ________ old things and we learnt a lot about farming in the old days. It is a ________ place.
5 Have you read Garcia's latest novel? I found it ________. I couldn't put it down.
6 Do you watch the nature programme on Channel 4? It's very ________. I thoroughly recommend it.
7 My sister is going hang gliding. I think it's very dangerous, but she says it's really ________.
8 Do you know, I spent ages trying to get through to your office the other day. The line was always engaged. It was absolutely ________!

Exercise 4

The boss at a factory is worried about complaints and falling standards of work, so he dictates a notice to his secretary. Use '*must*' + '*be*' + past participle (eg *must be done*) to complete the notice.

do	obtain
stop	wear
achieve	inspect
eliminate	take

MEMO
To: All office staff   Date: 30 May
From: John Bridges

We have received too many complaints. There have been too many mistakes. Something *must be done* to improve the standard of work.

1 All work ________ by a supervisor.
2 All errors ________.
3 Permission ________ before new work is started.
4 All possible care ________ to prevent damage.
5 Safety hats and glasses ________ when working on equipment.
6 Higher standards ________ – or we lose our jobs.

Exercise 5

Report this conservation

Example:

I've cooked dinner. *Yolanda said she had cooked dinner.*

Yolanda I've cooked dinner.
Rob And I've bought some wine.
Howard I bought some white wine yesterday. It's in the fridge.
Rob Well, I bought some red wine.
Howard That's fine. We'll have white wine for the fish and red wine for the steak.
Yolanda Well, I've got news for both of you. I haven't cooked any fish and I haven't cooked any steak.
Lisa So we're having a vegetarian meal today.
Rob That's all right. Wine is a vegetarian drink.

REVISION EXERCISES 13

Exercise 1

Check the order of the adjectives in these sentences. Two of the sentences are correct and four are incorrect. Re-write the sentences that are wrong.

Examples:

Rob's ex-girlfriend has got funny, little, blue eyes. ( )
Howard advised Rob to buy a heavy, round, iron, large cooking pot. (X)
Howard advised Rob to buy a large, round, heavy, iron cooking pot.

1 Jack owns an Italian, red, beautiful, old sports car. ( )
2 Lisa is reading an interesting, new, English novel. ( )
3 Yolanda has just bought herself a silk, Chinese expensive blouse. ( )
4 Last night Meg and Howard went to see an American excellent, new film, starring a young, Swedish, handsome actor. ( )
5 Rob found an old, brown, woollen jumper in the cupboard. ( )
6 Geoffrey and Dorothy have bought Suzy a Japanese, new, remarkable camera. ( )

Exercise 2

On their way to visit Dave's sister in Brighton, Suzy and Dave stopped for breakfast at a roadside café. They weren't very pleased with the food or the service. Change the comments below into exclamations.

Examples:

The service is slow.	*What slow service!*
The jukebox is noisy.	*What a noisy jukebox!*

1 This table is dirty. __________
2 The bread is dry. __________
3 This bacon is salty. __________
4 This sausage is greasy. __________
5 This food is terrible. __________
6 The milk is sour. __________
7 The waitress is lazy. __________
8 This is an expensive bill. __________

Exercise 3

Match up these sentences and join them using 'in order to' or 'to'.

Example:

Meg went to Florida. She wanted to attend the Oceanographic Conference.

Meg went to Florida a few months ago in order to attend the Oceanographic Conference.

1 Dave has borrowed the newspaper.
2 Suzy is attending classes in accountancy.
3 Yolanda is learning German.
4 Jack bought a present last week.

a) He wanted to send it to one of his girlfriends.
b) She wants to improve her job prospects.
c) He wants to check what is on television tonight.
d) She'd like to do a photo trip to Germany.

Using the same pattern, write endings for these sentences.

5 I bought this knife __________
6 He phoned me __________
7 We invited them __________
8 You wanted to wear that suit __________
9 She wrote him the letter __________

Exercise 4

Use the words in the table to make five sentences.

Examples:

If you want to learn Spanish, you should go to Spain.
If you want to speak Greek, you shouldn't go to Portugal.

learn	Greek	don't go to Portugal
speak	Spanish	go to Spain
arrive	a lasting suntan	don't go to the Roadside Inn
eat	on time	go on a shopping trip to Paris
save	good food	leave immediately
buy	money	sunbathe for short periods each day
get	smart clothes	open a deposit account at the bank

Now write endings for these sentences. Use the same pattern.

1 If your friend likes peace and quiet, he should ____________

2 If they want to enjoy themselves, they ____________

3 If she likes art, ____________

4 If you want to have a seat on the train, ____________

5 If they like city life, ____________

Exercise 5

A Complete the sentences using the words in the lists below.

learn	cigarettes
eat	polo
climb	difficult languages
jog	rich food
give up	serious novels
play	long distances
read	mountains

Example:

Learning difficult languages is a challenge.

1 ____________ is a dangerous pastime.

2 ____________ is an expensive hobby.

3 ____________ makes people irritable.

4 ____________ can hurt your feet.

5 ____________ makes me fall asleep.

6 ____________ is a problem if you're on a diet.

B Can you think of ways to finish these sentences?

1 Taking the lift ____________

2 Watching television ____________

3 Taking exams ____________

4 Choosing new clothes ____________

5 Spending money ____________

REVISION EXERCISES 14

Exercise 1

Read the following advertisement for 'ARTworld Holidays'.

ARTworld Holidays: we offer a complete programme of visits to museums and art galleries in major European art centres. Prices include entry fees and a complete programme of lectures from experts. Further details on request from: ARTworld, Maddox Street, London, W1R 9AF

	Madrid	Rome	Paris	Amsterdam	Venice
1 week	£150	£200	£200	£190	£220
2 weeks	£280	£375	£375	£360	£410
3 weeks	£400	£530	£530	£510	£600

a) Now give the questions for the following answers, using the same patterns:

Example:
£375

How much would I pay if I stayed in Paris for two weeks?

or *How much would it cost me if I stayed in Paris for two weeks?*

1 £150 **2** £510 **3** £600 **4** £280 **5** £220

b) In pairs, ask and answer questions as follows:

A: *How much would I pay if I stayed in Amsterdam for three weeks?*
B: *You'd pay £510.*

Exercise 2

Read the dialogue, and finish John's story.

Ann What's the matter with you? You look worn out.
John I am. I went to that keep fit class . . . with Walton, the new instructor.
Ann What happened?
John Well, first he made us run around the track.

Now look at the pictures and continue John's story using 'He made . . .' and words such as 'next', 'after that' etc.

Exercise 3

Remember:

If you say 'what happened next' use the Past Simple.
If you say 'what was happening at a certain time' use the Past Continuous.

Put in the correct form of the verb in the following passage.

Ann And where were you last night? We waited at the Queens Head till 9.

Bill I'm sorry. I went round to John's place at about 8. He (1 watch) a programme about dolphins. I (2 ask) him to come out, but he didn't want to. So I (3 decide) to go to the pub by myself. But while I (4 go) down London Road, I (5 meet) Joanne.

Ann Joanne!

Bill Yes, she (6 read) a newspaper. She almost (7 walk) into me.

Ann How interesting for you! What (8 she-wear)?

Bill I can't remember. But the funny thing is this. When she (9 walk) into me, she (10 read) her horoscope. It said she would meet an old friend unexpectedly!

Ann I suppose it said 'Romance on the Horizon' as well!

Exercise 4

Look at the pictures and make sentences as in the example.

1

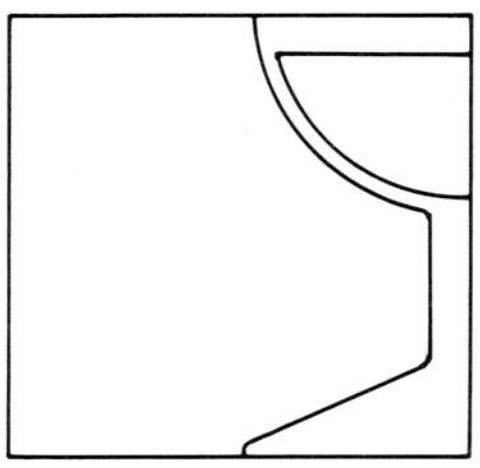

2

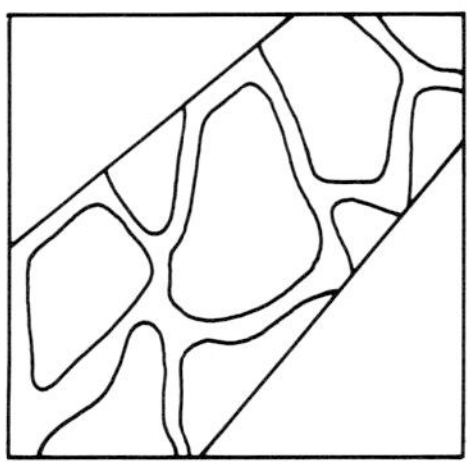

3

4

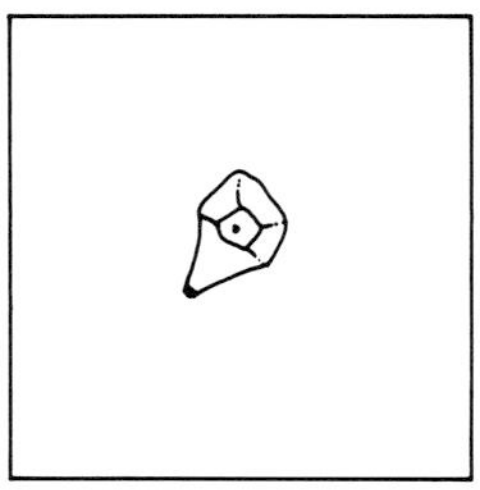

5

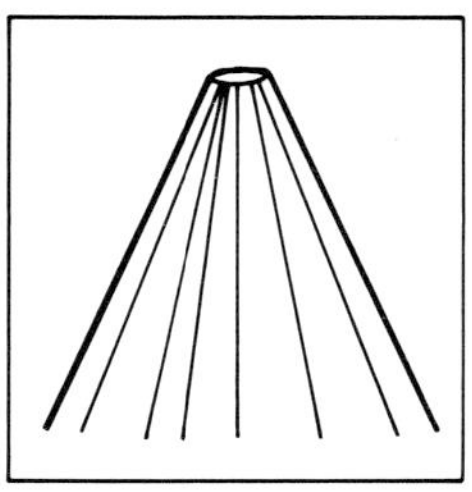

6

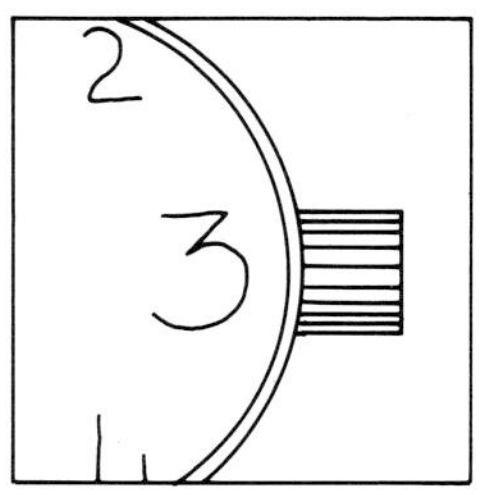

Example:

1 *It looks like a glass of wine.*

REVISION EXERCISES 15

Exercise 1

Solve these problems.

1 Meg ordered a new computer. The price was £3500. But the bill she received was £236 more than she had expected. How much was the bill?
2 Yolanda bought a new camera. She was lucky. It cost her £160 less than she had expected. It cost her £680. He much had she expected to pay?
3 We were unfortunate. Our flight to San Antonio was scheduled to take ten hours, but it took eleven and a half hours. How much longer was the flight than we had anticipated?
4 We went to a long film last night. We had expected it to finish at 11 o'clock. In fact, it was exactly 38 minutes longer than we had anticipated. What time did the film actually finish?
5 Lisa was late. She walked from town. She had expected to take thirty minutes. She left town at four o'clock and she arrived at the yacht at ten minutes past five. How much longer had her journey taken than she had expected?

Now complete sentences for each of the items below.

Example:

My journey to work usually takes twenty minutes.
Yesterday, I left home at 7 o'clock and arrived at work at 8.30.

Your journey took you one hour ten minutes longer than you had anticipated.

1 The drive to London normally takes an hour. Yesterday, we left at 10.00 and finally arrived at 12.30.
2 Last time I dined there, the bill came to £130 for four people. Last night we paid £155 for dinner for four.
3 I ordered a new car two months ago. The price was £10000. Now it is ready, and the price is £10 980.
4 Yolanda ordered some films. The price was $300. She normally pays $270 for the same films.
5 Jack rented a car. The advertised rate was $50 per day. It cost him $350 for five days.

Exercise 2

Write sentences using the words below. Follow the example.

Example:

Where. Go. A Policeman.

If you don't know where to go, ask a policeman.

1 What. See. A guide.
2 When. Leave. An attendant.
3 Who. Ask. The teacher.
4 What. Buy. The assistant.
5 What. Catch. A station attendant.
6 What. Do. The supervisor.
7 How. Do. The instructor.
8 Where. Pay. The manager.

Write three sentences of this pattern, advising visitors to your workplace, town or country.

Exercise 3

Complete the sentences below. Choose from this list.

a doctor	a mechanic	a travel agent
a librarian	a dictionary	

1 You have a bad headache. You want some treatment.
The best person to go to *is a doctor.*
2 You want to book a vacation. You want some advice.
The best person to ask . . .
3 Your car isn't running properly. You want to have it fixed.
The best person to fix . . .
4 You can't find a library book. You want some help.
The best person to ask . . .
5 You can't understand a new word. You want to find the meaning.
The best place to look . . .

Exercise 4

Make up sentences from the table below.

Example:

An Indian restaurant isn't the best place to go for spaghetti.

A disco An Indian restaurant A French restaurant A pub A museum A vegetarian restaurant A bookshop	isn't the best place to go is the best place to go	for	a dance. fish and chips. a beef steak. a quiet evening out. a newspaper. spaghetti. an amusing evening out.

Make up four sentences like these to give advice to someone visiting your town or country.

Exercise 5

Complete the questions below, using words from the list.

a holiday
a break
a chance
a rest
a drink
a look

1 Why don't you take ________? You might be lucky.
2 Why don't you take ________? You should go away for a while.
3 Why don't you take ________ at this book? You'll find it very informative.
4 Why don't you take ________? You can go outside for a few minutes.
5 Why don't you take ________? You look very tired.
6 Why don't you take ________? I'm going to make a cup of tea.

Exercise 6

Complete the sentence pairs below.

Example:

A: You seem (jog) a lot these days.
B: That's because I (try) to lose weight.

A: *You seem to be jogging a lot these days.*
B: *That's because I'm trying to lose weight.*

1 A: You seem (work) very late these days.
B: That's because I (take) some time off next month.

2 A: Bob seems (train) a lot these days.
B: That's because he (run) in the marathon next month.

3 A: Ann seems (save) a lot of money these days.
B: That's because she (go) to New Zealand at Christmas.

4 A: You seem (buy) a lot of food today.
B: That's because people (come) to dinner this evening.

5 A: Helen seems (go) to London a lot these days.
B: That's because she (take) a course at the Royal College of Art.

REVISION EXERCISES 16

Exercise 1

Remember:

I write three or four letters every week.
I'm busy. I'm writing a letter.
I'm writing a lot of letters these days.
I'm writing to John tomorrow.
I've written a letter to Jane.

Complete the letter from Patricia to her parents by putting the verb in brackets into the Present Simple, the Present Continuous or the Present Perfect.

Dear Mum and Dad,

I'm sorry that I (1 not-write) to you for such a long time. I (2 work) a lot these days. Every day, even Sunday, I (3 get) up very early and I usually (4 start) studying at 7 o'clock.

I (5 do) the exams next Thursday and Friday. After that, I (6 go) on holiday. Joanne (7 come) with me, I hope. Anyway, I (8 write) to her, and now I (9 wait) for her reply. She usually (10 answer) as soon as she gets a letter.

I hope you are well. Love to everybody.

Patricia

Exercise 2

Look at John's diary for next Tuesday. He's very busy. Answer the questions and say what he will have done by a certain time, and also say what he will do at a certain time.

1 By 10.15 am John will have __________.
2 At 10.30 he will __________.
3 At 12.30 he __________.
4 By 2.15 __________.
5 At 2.30 __________.
6 At 4.30 __________.
7 By 6.15 __________.
8 At 6.30 __________.

am
9.00 to 10.00 Finish my report for Finance Division.
10.30 Go to Paddington Station to take 11.15 train to Oxford.
12.30 Lunch in Oxford (Randolph Hotel) with Mr Tada (Japan Piston Company) Finish by 2.15

pm
2.30 Visit Cowley office with Mr Tada
4.30 Tea
5.00 to 6.00 Meeting with JPC Personnel Manager
6.30 Train back to London

Exercise 3

Respond to the situation as in the example.

Example:

Mary didn't come, because we didn't ask her.
Mary would have come if we had asked her.

1 Jane didn't stop, because she didn't see you.
Jane would have stopped if ________.
2 Mike didn't lend you £5, because you didn't ask him.
Mike would have ________.
3 Ron's car didn't crash. He stopped in time.
Ron's car would have ________.
4 I didn't lend you my umbrella. I didn't take it with me.
I would ________.
5 I didn't talk to Maria because I didn't see her.
I ________.
6 Jack didn't photocopy the papers because he didn't have enough time.
________.
7 Lisa didn't telephone John last night. Her phone was out of order.
________.
8 Bob didn't watch the film last night. His TV was out of order.
________.

Exercise 4

Think about a period in history. Write five sentences about the life you would have had if you had lived then. Say what you would have done, and what you would not have done.

If I had lived in ________ I would have ________

(Continue with 'I would have ________' Do not repeat 'If I had lived . . .' each time.)

Some periods in history: in prehistoric times
in the Iron Age
in the Middle Ages
three hundred years ago
eighty years ago
etc.

Verbs to wear: I would have worn.
to eat: eaten
to drink: drunk
to carry: carried
to drive: driven
to ride: ridden
etc.

APPENDIX

The Noun Phrase

Nouns can be classified as follows:

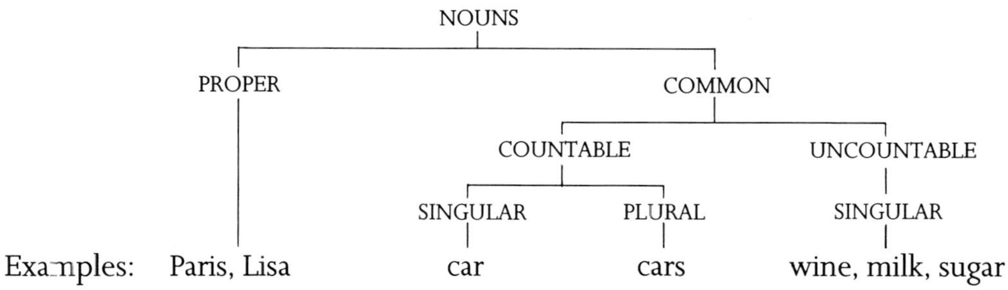

All uncountable nouns are singular. Countable nouns can be either singular or plural.

There are three main parts in the noun phrase, of which parts 1 and 2 are optional. Part 3 must be filled.

1	2								3
Article/ Quantifier	Opinion	Size	Shape	Weight	Age	Colour & Design	Adjective of Nationality	Material	NOUN
a/an	nice	small	round	heavy	old	green	Portuguese	gold	cross
the	beautiful	large	square	light	new	purple	Indian	silk	scarf
some, any	luxurious					black	German		car
many	fantastic								
a lot of	excellent								
a few									
a little									
few									

In position 1, the following can be used as follows:

Singular Countable Nouns	Plural Countable Nouns	Uncountable Nouns
a/an	the	the
the	many	some
	a lot of	any
	a few	a lot of
	few	a little

In addition to items *before* the noun, there can be items *after* the noun:

1	2	3	4
the	tall young	*man*	with the long blond hair
the	expensive German	*car*	in the garage
some	cheap	*souvenirs*	from America
the		*person*	who telephoned yesterday

It is possible to have items from all four positions, and it is possible to have up to eight items from position 2. Such long noun phrases are very rare and are very difficult to understand. So, do not choose more than two or three items from position 2.

The Verb Phrase

Verbs are of two types:

VERB	
REGULAR e.g. *play*	IRREGULAR e.g. *go*

The verb has the following forms:

Form	Usual Name	Example
Verb	Infinitive	*play, go*
Verb + *ing*	Present Participle	*playing, going*
Verb + *s*	3rd person singular Present Tense	*plays, goes*
Verb + *ed*	Past Tense	*played, went*
Verb + *ed*	Past Participle	*played, gone*

Here are the verb forms covered in *Formula Two*:

Verb Forms

Present Perfect Continuous

I have been working
You have been working
She/he/it has been working
Etc.

Have I been working?
Have you been working?
Has she/he/it been working?
Etc.

I haven't been working
You haven't been working
She/he/it hasn't been working
Etc.

Haven't I been working?
Haven't you been working?
Hasn't she/he/it been working?
Etc.

Perfect with 'will'

I will (I'll) have worked
You will (you'll) have worked
Etc.

Will I have worked?

Will you have worked?
Etc.

I won't (will not) have worked
You won't (will not) have worked
Etc.

Won't I have worked? (Will I not have worked? *unusual*)
Won't you have worked? (Will you not have worked? *unusual*)
Etc.

Modal Verbs

Note: The form is the same for all persons. There is no 3rd person 's'.

I may go
May I go?

I may not go
Mayn't I go? (May I not go? *unusual*)

I might go
Might I go?

I might not go
Mightn't I go? (Might I not go? *unusual*)

I will go
Will I go?

I will not go (I won't go)
Won't I go? (Will I not go? *unusual*)

I would go
Would I go?

I would not go (I wouldn't go)
Wouldn't I go? (Would I not go? *unusual*)

I shall (I'll) go
Shall I go?

I shall not go (I shan't go)
Shan't I go? (Shall I not go? *unusual*)

I should (I'd) go
Should I go?

I should not go (I shouldn't go)
Shouldn't I go?

I can go
Can I go?

I can't go
Can't I go?

I could go
Could I go?

I couldn't go
Couldn't I go? (Could I not go? *unusual*)

Passive

Present Simple

I am (I'm) rejected
You are (You're) rejected
She/he/it is (She's, he's, it's) rejected
Etc.

I am not (I'm not) rejected
You are not (You're not/You aren't) rejected
She/he/it is not (isn't) rejected
Etc.

Am I rejected?
Are you rejected?
Is she/he/it rejected?
Etc.

Aren't I rejected? (Am I not rejected? *unusual*)
Aren't you rejected?
Isn't she/he/it rejected?
Etc.

Present Continuous

I am (I'm) being interviewed
Am I being interviewed?
Etc.

I am not (I'm not) being interviewed
Aren't I being interviewed? (Am I not being interviewed? *unusual*)
Etc.

Past

I was interviewed
Was I interviewed?
Etc.

I was not (wasn't) interviewed
Wasn't I interviewed? (Was I not interviewed? *unusual*)
Etc.

Passive with modal verbs

These bags must be inspected.
Must these bags be inspected?
Etc.

These bags must not be inspected.
Mustn't these bags be inspected?
Etc.

(Other modals operate in the same way.)

Sentences with 'If'

1 Present (Simple, Continuous or Perfect) after 'If':

If you *like* films, we *can go* to the cinema.
If you *ask* John, he *will* (he'll) *help* you.
If you *visit* Paris, *go* to the Eiffel Tower.
If he *doesn't arrive*, I *am* (I'm) *having* lunch without him.
If she *has* (she's) *arrived*, we *can ask* her.

2 Past Simple after 'If':

If I *were* you, I *would* (I'd) *run*. (Alternative: If I *was* you, I'd *run*.)
If I *saw* Lisa, I *would* (I'd) *feel* happy.
If we *changed* our plans, we *might avoid* trouble.
If we *had enough* money, we *could go* on holiday.

3 Past Perfect after 'If':

If I *had* (I'd) *seen* Meg, I *would* (I'd) *have helped* her.
If you *had* (you'd) *asked* me, I *might have helped* you.
If you *had* (you'd) *arrived* early, I *could have helped* you.

If they *had* (they'd) *wanted* us to help, they *should have asked* us.
If you *hadn't helped* me, I *wouldn't have finished*.

Tag Questions

He sings, *doesn't he?*	He doesn't sing, *does he?*
He sang, *didn't he?*	He didn't sing, *did he?*
He's singing, *isn't he?*	He isn't singing, *is he?*
He was singing, *wasn't he?*	He wasn't singing, *was he?*
He has sung, *hasn't he?*	He hasn't sung, *has he?*
He had sung, *hadn't he?*	He hadn't sung, *had he?*
He can sing, *can't he?*	He can't sing, *can he?*
He could sing, *couldn't he?*	He couldn't sing, *could he?*

(All other modals operate in the same way in tag questions.)

Indirect Speech

General rule. After a past verb of reporting:

Direct Speech		**Indirect Speech**
Present Simple	*becomes* →	Past Simple
Present Continuous		Past Continuous
Present Perfect		Past Perfect
Past Simple		Past Perfect
Past Perfect		Past Perfect
Past Continuous		Past Perfect Continuous

Statements:

'I *am* very happy,' Pete said. Pete said that he *was* very happy.

Commands:

'*Move* the boxes!' Howard said to Pete. Howard told Pete *to move* the boxes.

Questions:

'Is Rob *coming?*' Jack asked. Jack asked if Rob *was coming*.

'*Can* I *help?*' Lisa asked. Lisa asked if she *could help*.

VOCABULARY

This vocabulary list gives the number of the lesson where each word first occurs in the Student's Book. The words with an asterisk* first occur in the exercises of the lesson indicated.

A

a matter of life and death (*idiom*) (43)
aboard (12)
accept (v) (10)
access (61)
accommodation (42)
according (16)
account (52)
accountant (54)
action (47)
address (14)
administration (41)
admiration (51)
admire * (v) (44)
admit (v) (41)
advanced (4)
adventure (7)
adventurous * (7)
advertize (v) (9)
advertizement (7)
advise (v) (47)
Africa (9)
afters * (38)
afterwards (62)
age (8)
agency (10)
agent (8)
ahead (36)
aide (47)
alcohol (12)
Alexandria * (52)
alias (53)
alone (12)
alright (46)
Alsatian * (27)
also * (3)
although (43)
amateur (26)
amazing (24)
Amazon * (30)
amber (23)
ambitious (7)
ambulance (27)
America * (1)
American (59)
amount (3)
amusing * (31)
an arm and a leg (*idiom*) (59)
ancestor (46)
anchor (12)
angel (56)
anger * (24)
annoyed (17)
annoying * (57)
Antarctic * (37)
anticipated (57)
Aotearoa (37)
appeal (57)
appear * (v) (61)
appearance * (42)
applicant * (4)
application (7)
apply (v) (4)
appointment * (19)
appreciate (v) (19)
approach (v) (36)
approximately (62)
Arabic * (9)
Argentine (4)
argue (v) (17)
argument (7)
arm (54)
army (22)
arrest (v) (22)
arson (34)
as (18)
Athens * (52)
athletic (1)
at least (11)
Atlantic (13)
atmosphere * (36)
attack (27)
attention (34)
attitude (18)
attract (v) (51)
Auckland (37)
audio * (11)
Aussie (37)
Australia (9)
Australian (1)
Austria * (12)
authentic (38)
automatic (5)
available (39)
average * (1)
avoid * (v) (11)
aware (2)
away (43)
awhile (16)

B

babysitting (54)
back (35)
backwards (54)
Bahia Grande (34)
balcony * (37)
bang (48)
Bangkok (39)
Barbados (3)
Barcelona * (52)
bargain (v) (42)
baseball * (1)
basic (42)
basically (51)
basketball * (28)
Bay of Biscay (47)
be able (v) (6)
be born * (v) (6)
be certain (v) (7)
be in touch (v) (47)
be interested in * (v) (1)
beard * (31)
beef (13)
beer * (12)
begin (v) (18)
behalf (62)
belong * (v) (49)
belongings (62)
below * (1)
Berlin * (52)
bet (v) (17)
Big Apple (20)
bike * (37)
bikini * (7)
biologist * (27)
Birmingham * (11)
birthday (5)
bite * (v) (27)

E

F

M

N

O

P

Q

R

S

T

CONTENTS CHART

LESSON	GRAMMAR POINT	EXAMPLE	FUNCTION
1	'–*ing*' verb form after '*like*' '*enjoy*' '*be interested in*'	*I enjoy eating it.*	Asking for and giving information about people
2	'*used to*' + verb	*We used to be a busy organization.*	Describing past situations and routines
3	'*wanted to*' + verb	*We wanted to go there.*	Reporting past wishes
4	Present Perfect of '*to be*'	*How long have you been a photographer?*	Asking for and giving information about people
5	Defining relative clauses	*They're the photos that we took on Friday.*	Identifying specific things or people
6	(i) Modal '*will*' with future reference (ii) Present Simple with future reference in subordinate clauses of time (after '*when, as soon as*')	*We'll make our selection when Meg returns.*	Making plans
7	Modal '*should*' + verb	*You should make an application.*	Giving advice
8	Past Perfect in contrast with Past Simple	*Peter left me. He had got married.*	Reporting past events (out of chronological sequence)
9	(i) Negative tags with '*be*' (ii) Present Continuous	*He's very generous, isn't he?* *I'm preparing a list.*	Inviting agreement. Talking about activities in an on-going period of time (not necessarily activities which are 'happening now')
10	Present Perfect Continuous	*I haven't been eating properly.*	Eliciting and providing information
11	(i) Conditional sentences (1) (ii) Comparative and superlative of adjectives	*If you talk like that, this voyage will be a disaster.* *It's longer.* *My cabin's the biggest.*	Advising Outlining outcomes for given conditions Describing things
12	(i) Passive verbs, Present Simple (ii) Question tags, positive	*My letters are returned.* *Robert doesn't want to stay, does he?*	Describing situations and processes Inviting agreement with negative proposition
13	(i) '*going to*' + verb (ii) Question tags, negative (iii) Comparison of adjectives with '*more*' and '*most*'	*You're going to have an exciting time.* *You like salt beef sandwiches, don't you?* '*the most exciting time of your life*'	Talking about the future Inviting agreement with positive proposition Describing things and events
14	(i) Conditional sentences (1) [c.f. 11] (ii) Present Progressive with future reference	*If you contact him, he'll help you.* *If you stop in Recife, contact Carlos Couto.* *I'm going to the pub.*	Making suggestions, and giving advice Talking about future plans

LESSON	GRAMMAR POINT	EXAMPLE	FUNCTION
15	(i) Questions with 'think' (ii) Indirect questions in the past	*Do you think they're quarrelling?* *She asked if you could send more money.*	Conjecturing about events Reporting
16	(i) Modal '*may*' (ii) Comparison of inequality with '*not as . . . as*' Negative questions	*There may be more.* *It isn't as bad as it was in Cape Horn.* *Why don't we go south?*	Expressing possibility Expressing comparisons Making suggestions
17	(i) Reported commands in the past (ii) '*too*' + adjective + '*to*' + verb	*He told me to stop wasting time.* *The boxes were too heavy to lift.*	Reporting the past Describing
18	(i) Modal '*will*' and clauses with '*when*', '*as soon as*' (ii) Predeterminers '*some of . . .*', '*all of . . .*'	*I'll be glad when we reach the USA.* *Robert ate all of the biscuits.*	Talking about the future Specifying quantity
19	Conditional sentences (2)	*If I were you, I'd relax.*	Seeking and giving advice
20	Modal '*might*' + verb	*She might eat you!*	Conjecturing as part of giving advice; warning
21	Past Perfect. ('*had*' + past participle)	*Someone had put them there.*	Narrating past events and indicating temporal relationship
22	(i) Passive, Past Simple (ii) Determiner '*enough*'	*All of us were interviewed.* *We haven't got enough flour.*	Reporting on past events Specifying quantity available
23	(i) Modal '*should*' with '*have*' + past participle (ii) '*remember*' + '*to*' + verb '*forget*' + '*to*' + verb	*He shouldn't have said that.*	Attributing causes, blaming Recalling the past
24	(i) Indirect questions with '*wonder*' (ii) Predeterminers: '*a lot of*', '*a good deal of*'	*I wonder if they'll see us.* *a good deal of fine weather*	Conjecturing Quantifying
25	(i) Construction with verb '*wish*' (ii) Conditional sentences (2) (c.f. 19)	*I wish I was wrong.* *If I was there, I'd find the truth.*	Expressing desires Talking about hypothetical situations
26	(i) Modal '*could*' + verb (ii) Link verb '*manage*' + '*to*' + verb	*I could repair a boat when I was twelve.* *We managed to complete the journey.*	Describing past abilities and achievements
27	Defining relative clauses (c.f 5)	*The girl who's looking at the camera.*	Specifying and identifying
28	Adverbs of frequency and manner	*He sometimes behaves childishly.*	Describing people and situations
29	(i) Modal '*would*' (ii) Predeterminer '*both of*'	*I'd like a steak.* *both of them*	Inviting and requesting Quantifying
30	Conditional sentences (2) (c.f. 19, 25)	*If we changed our route, we might avoid difficulties.*	Making suggestions, giving advice
31	Prepositional phrases '*with . . .*' '*in . . .*'	*the chap with the funny hat*	Describing
32	Constructions with '*it*' ('dummy it')	*It's lucky that we're in a petrol station.*	Discussing situations
33	Construction with '*until*'	*They'll continue until they get some answers.*	Talking about future arrangements

LESSON	GRAMMAR POINT	EXAMPLE	FUNCTION
34	Indefinite pronouns. '*Everyone/–body/thing* *no one/–body/–thing*'	*Everybody is tired.*	Quantifying
35	'*must*' and '*have to*' + verb	*You'll have to hurry.*	Stating necessity
36	Passive, Present Continuous	*The islands are being liberated.*	Talking about what's happening
37	(i) Indefinite adverbials '*somewhere, anywhere, nowhere*' (ii) Indefinite pronouns '*someone, anyone*'	*There are sharks everywhere.*	Describing places
38	Passive, Present Simple	*Stones are placed on the wood.*	Describing processes
39	'*had better*' and '*would rather*'	*You'd better ask first.* *I'd rather go to the countryside.*	Giving advice Expressing preference
40	Conditional sentences (3)	*If I'd seen her, I would have asked her.*	Reviewing past events with unfulfilled hypotheses
41	(i) Repeat patterns with '*so . . .*', '*neither . . .*' (ii) Conditional sentences (1) with Present Progressive	*So am I. Neither am I.* *If he doesn't come, I'm leaving.*	Expressing agreement Talking about future plans
42	(i) Verbs of sensation (ii) '*too*' + adjective + '*for*' + (*someone*) + '*to*' + verb	*The earth smells fresh. Too hot for tourists to eat.*	Describing places and states
43	(i) Phrasal verbs (ii) Conjunctions '*although*' and '*because*'	*Did you pick them up?* *Although I like your sister, I don't want to go.*	Indicating contrasts and reasons
44	(i) Modal '*must*' and '*should*' (c.f. 35) (ii) Indefinites: '*someone/ no one/anyone* *Something/nothing/anything* *somewhere/nowhere/anywhere*'	*We must leave!*	Expressing necessity and obligation
45	Reported speech with '*promise*' '*promise that . . .*' '*promise to . . .*'	*They promised to deliver the supplies.*	Reporting promises and intentions
46	'*so*' + adjective	*It is so full of interesting things.*	Describing things and justifying one's views
47	'*Must*' + '*be*' + past participle	*They must be eliminated.*	Giving instructions
48	(i) Reported speech (with Past perfect) Structures with '*say*' and '*tell*'	*He said that he had come to take photographs.* *He told me that he had seen a suspicious character.*	Reporting what was said
49	(i) Order of adjectives (ii) '*What a*' + noun	*funny, little, blue eyes.* *What a great place!*	Describing Exclaiming
50	Verbs of measurement '*last*', '*weigh*', '*cost*'	*The performance lasted an hour.*	Reporting and describing
51	Infinitive of purpose ('*to*' and '*in order to*')	*I worked hard to get my degree*	Expressing and reporting purpose
52	(i) Conditional sentences with Present Tense and '*should*' (ii) Verb '*–ing*' as subject or object	*If you like spaces, you should visit the desert.* *Photographing dolphins is difficult.*	Giving advice Describing habits, events

LESSON	GRAMMAR POINT	EXAMPLE	FUNCTION
53	Conditional sentences (2) (c.f. 19, 25, 30)	*He would help you, if you asked him.*	Advising
54	(i) '*what/how to*' + verb (ii) . . '*make*' + noun + verb . .	*Dan showed me what to do.* *The doctor made me do it.*	Reporting
55	Constructions after '*seem*' and '*remember*'	*They seem to be stopping.* *I remember Jack telephoning.*	Describing and reporting
56	(i) Past Continuous (ii) to '*look like*'	*Jack was repairing the boat.* *She looks like a French naval boat.*	Describing situations Describing similar things
57	Comparative construction after '*take*', '*last*'	*It took one week longer than we had planned.*	Reporting
58	'*Wh–*' clause as object of verb	*I don't know who to ask.*	Expressing knowledge or lack of knowledge
59	(i) Superlative adjective with '*to*' + verb and conditional (ii) Superlative adjective with '*to*' + verb and '*for . . .*'	*It's the best place to choose if you want good jazz.* *It's the best place to go for a good meal.*	Giving advice Making recommendations
60	Phrases with '*take*'	*I'm going to take a look.*	
61	Contrast of Present Simple, Present Progressive, Present Perfect	*I haven't seen her before.* *I see she's using a word processor.*	Expressing views
62	Conjunctions '*although*', '*so*', '*but*', '*because*'	*Although they had locked everything, the door was open.*	Expressing logical relationships between events or actions
63	Future Perfect	*They'll have come to some conclusions.*	Expressing inferences
64	Conditional sentences (3) (c.f. 40)	*If you hadn't helped us, we wouldn't have defeated the government.*	Talking about the past Conjecturing

REVISION LESSONS

Each revision lesson covers four lessons in the book, as follows:

REVISION LESSON 1 : LESSONS 1 – 4
REVISION LESSON 2 : LESSONS 5 – 8
REVISION LESSON 3 : LESSONS 9 – 12
REVISION LESSON 4 : LESSONS 13 – 16
REVISION LESSON 5 : LESSONS 17 – 20
REVISION LESSON 6 : LESSONS 21 – 24
REVISION LESSON 7 : LESSONS 25 – 28
REVISION LESSON 8 : LESSONS 29 – 32
REVISION LESSON 9 : LESSONS 33 – 36
REVISION LESSON 10 : LESSONS 37 – 40
REVISION LESSON 11 : LESSONS 41 – 44
REVISION LESSON 12 : LESSONS 45 – 48
REVISION LESSON 13 : LESSONS 49 – 52
REVISION LESSON 14 : LESSONS 53 – 56
REVISION LESSON 15 : LESSONS 57 – 60
REVISION LESSON 16 : LESSONS 61 – 64

First published 1990

Published by *MACMILLAN PUBLISHERS LIMITED*
London and Basingstoke

A CIP catalogue record for this book is available from the British Library.

ISBN 0–333–49194 7

Designed by Mike Brain
Typeset by Gecko Ltd, Bicester Oxon
Illustrations by Andrew Aloof and Associates, Jane Cheswright, Frank James and Nancy Sutcliffe

Produced by AMR for Macmillan Publishers Ltd

Printed in Singapore

Photographic Credits
t = top b = bottom l = left r = right c = centre

The authors and publishers wish to acknowledge with thanks, the following photographic sources: 6r, 15r, 25b, 27b, 43t, 44t, 56t, 70b, 76t, 78t, 80t, 88t, 92t, 93b, 94t, 100t, 102, 120t Picture point; 8t, 17r Colorsport; 35b, 59b, 83r, 123r Barnaby's Picture Library; 79b High Commissioner for New Zealand; 107l Anne Bolt; 107r Douglas Dickens

The publishers would also wish to acknowledge their thanks to Camper Nicholson (Yachts Ltd) for their help and guidance in providing illustration reference for this publication.